# Anton Mosimann ~naturally

# Anton Mosimann
# ~naturally

Photography by Tom Belshaw

EBURY PRESS
LONDON

To all those who love good food

First published in 1991 by Ebury Press
an imprint of the Random Century Group
Random Century House
20 Vauxhall Bridge Road
London SW1V 2SA

Second impression 1991

Edited by Susan Fleming
Designed by The Image
Photography by Tom Belshaw
Styling by Roisin Neild

British Library Cataloguing in Publication Data

Mosimann, Anton
Anton Mosimann – naturally!.
I. Title
641.5

ISBN 0-09-174959-X (paperback)
0-09-175275-2 (hardback)

Filmset in Baskerville by Tek Art Ltd,
Addiscombe, Croydon, Surrey
Printed and bound in Great Britain by
Butler & Tanner Ltd, Frome and London

# CONTENTS

# INTRODUCTION

In this book, and in the television series it accompanies, I have chosen to explore dishes using natural foods. By 'natural', I mean foods which have been grown or produced without too much interference – the young vegetable freshly pulled from a soil free of fertilisers, the fruit which has not been immersed in sugar in a can, and the flour which has not been so over-milled that nutrients have to be *added* to the bread made from it.

I have also chosen to explore dishes which exclude meat. More and more people are turning away from meat these days. In many cases this is due to the meat and poultry scares we have experienced lately (most due to an interference in natural processes), and often economy has much to do with it. For the majority, though, the primary incentive is health. A carefully designed meat-free diet – so long as it contains some protein in the form of fish or dairy produce – is generally believed to be healthier than one which contains the saturated fats of meat.

These are trends which we chefs are at last taking seriously, and a number of us have been working to create interesting dishes, exciting dishes, which utilise the best possible natural ingredients and which exclude meat. This has been made easier by the fact that in this country much better and more natural produce is once again available. Having become conscious of the disadvantages of mass production and processing – the frozen fish without texture, the vegetable bred to crop well but which lacks flavour – people are now buying from small suppliers who offer 'home-grown', 'free-range' and organic protein foods, fruits, vegetables and herbs.

Exploring all the possibilities has been very exhilarating. Cooking fish has always been a delight for me anyway, but experimenting with new combinations, with new flavours, with different foods that could replace meat, has been a revelation. The diversity of alternatives is so great that they make for a galaxy of sophisticated and flavourful dishes.

If ingredients are natural and good, they are full of flavour and nutrients, and it is this marriage that is essential and most valuable for those who are not eating meat. Even up to eight or ten years ago, a vegetarian or meat-free diet with its nut cutlets and meat substitutes was considered worthy but dull. I think there is absolutely no reason why any diet, let alone a meat-free one, should ever be dull or boring. I hope the following recipes will open people's eyes to the abundance of ways in which we can produce dishes excluding meat which are both exciting and healthy – which look good, taste good and *do* you good – and to do so easily at home. Even people who eat meat on a regular basis can become converted to a few meat-free meals once they are introduced to the flavours and textures of the dishes in the following chapters.

## THE INSPIRATIONS

My inspirations in the search for exciting and healthy meat-free recipes have been many. My own Central European upbringing has been one of the main influences. Switzerland is a country which produces some wonderful cheeses (and the best chocolate!), and I have used a number of interesting recipes that I remember from my childhood. It was in Switzerland, for instance, that I first became passionate about fish. These were inevitably, in a land-locked country, freshwater fish from lakes and rivers, and thus I was led to the cuisines of other Central European countries that utilised the same sorts of ingredients.

There are parallels without number in the cuisines of Switzerland, Austria, Hungary, Poland, Germany, Turkey, Yugoslavia, and Czechoslovakia. This central part of the continent had been over-run at different times throughout history by different conquerors and occupiers, and in each an element of culinary influence had taken hold, while an individuality unique to that country had been retained. The conquest-hungry Turks seem to have been most influential, introducing, for instance, coffee and *strudel* pastry; now the Austrians are supreme in the art of serving coffee, and the Hungarians in the making of *strudel*.

Following the recent political changes, we decided that it would be exciting to explore in a culinary sense where east meets west, and thus we went to Hungary. This flamboyant, agriculturally rich country sits virtually in the middle of the continental mass, and her cuisine is rich and diverse, exemplifying many of the characteristics of her neighbours, but with marginal individual accents. The main accent is rather more than marginal, for the principal feature of Hungarian cuisine is its use of paprika, the seasoning obtained from dried red sweet peppers. This plant was once again introduced by the Turks, but it is Hungary that has claimed it as her own; houses and farms are uniformly scarlet in the autumn with strings of pods hanging to dry in the sun.

It was in Hungary that I encountered thick vegetable soups served with *galuska* (dumplings) and fish soup made with carp from the Danube and flavoured with paprika. There they serve unusual dishes utilising pulses, grains and a variety of vegetables – pumpkins, marrows, peppers, kohlrabi – which are the sustenance of peasant cultures around the world when meat protein is scarce or too expensive.

Hungary, like many other of her neighbouring countries, has a form of pasta. It is in Italy, however, that pasta reigns supreme, and this was another of my influences. I worked there for a year and was fortunate enough to encounter real Italian cooking, sharing meals with my fellow chefs in their homes. Their mothers and wives would work all day, planning, marketing, preparing and cooking, for the evening meal. Pasta now is a 'fast' food in a sense, but it is a valuable one, providing energy-giving carbohydrate in any diet. With a few flavourful vegetables and some wonderful cheese, many exciting and healthy dishes can be created.

Another influence was the time I spent in Sweden, having fallen in love with a fish, the herring! The Swedes are masters of the herring art, and I learned a great deal. However, the principal spur in my fish education was the year I lived and worked in Japan. The Japanese diet consists primarily of seafood, and is acknowledged to be very healthy. Many of my fish dishes here have a very distinctive Japanese accent, which is now possible for us to achieve in this country because of the increasing availability of many Japanese products. These include soy sauce, *tamari* (fermented soy sauce), *miso* (a fermented soy and grain seasoning, used as condiment, soup starter or spread) and *tofu* (soy bean curd or 'cheese'). Fermented black beans, used in a few of the recipes throughout the book, are also a soy bean product. Soya is the only food of non-animal origin that contains complete protein.

I learned a great deal during my time in Japan, and also had a most enjoyable time talking to and cooking for Maki and Mideo Nakamura. Mideo, a trained chef, is setting up his own restaurant in Bayswater, London, and he and his wife, a banker and an excellent cook herself, contributed greatly to my understanding of their country's cuisine, and how it can be reproduced here.

If my inspirations started in Switzerland, so they culminated there too. Chocolate does not immediately equate with health in most people's minds, but there is nothing wrong with self-indulgence every now and again – perhaps on Sundays! I like a small slice of chocolate gâteau – a star at a British afternoon tea, one of my favourite meals – and a chocolate truffle as the final treat after a good dinner. Switzerland is famed for its chocolate, and I wanted to find out more about it. My trip to Suchard was a revelation, learning about *couverture*, the chocolate used in most chocolate specialities, and I also profited a great deal by watching and listening to Willi Graf at the Bellevue Palace Hotel in Bern.

Switzerland, as I said, is also a country of cheese, and I was taught very early to handle cheese, to judge its texture, taste, ripeness etc. Switzerland's most famous cheese dish must be fondue – that combination of local cheeses melted with Kirsch, after which ski-ing seems so much easier! As a young chef in Mexico during the 1968 Olympics, I watched a lone gentleman order fondue for lunch on a hot day (when it arrived, he thought it was a good, thick soup!), and my nationalistic hackles rose. But I felt some sadness too. Fondue should not only be eaten in the cold of winter, but it is also a dish that invites sitting around a table, sharing with family and friends. That, widening the parameters, is what eating should *always* be about, and I hope that this book, with its emphasis on natural foods, will help bring you together with your friends in happy and healthy companionship!

## A FEW DIETARY BASICS

To survive, people need the essential nutrients of proteins, fats, carbohydrates, vitamins, minerals, trace elements and water.

**Protein** is made up of various arrangements of small organic chemicals called amino acids, and of the twenty found in man, nine cannot be synthesised by the human body and must be supplied. Meat, fish, eggs, milk, cheese, yoghurt etc contain all these amino acids, therefore are complete proteins – as is the soya bean.

However, many other foods, although they do not contain all the essential amino acids, are also valuable protein sources. The 'incomplete' protein foods include grains (wheat, rye, oats, barley, millet etc, and all produce made from them), pulses or légumes (dried beans, peas, lentils etc), nuts and seeds. By combining complete proteins with incomplete proteins, or one incomplete protein with another, the amino acids of one can complement and supplement the amino acids of the other, thereby improving the quality and quantity of the protein content of the dish concerned. This 'combining' is not at all difficult, and is a concept which is basic to and instinctive in many cultures and cuisines where meat plays a minimal part in the diet. Think of the Italian combination of pasta, pizza or polenta with cheese, the bean and rice dishes of the Caribbean and South America, the Greek dip *hummus* which is a combination of pulse, chickpeas, and sesame seeds. Even just having milk and a muesli for breakfast or accompanying a thick vegetable soup with some whole-grain bread (and perhaps a slice of cheese) accomplishes the same nutritional purpose.

**Fats** are visible or invisible, but a proportion of fat is as vital as protein for the good working of the body. The visible fats are oils, butter, margarine etc, and the fat actually on meat. Less visible are the fats contained in animal products such as eggs, milk and cheese, in nuts and seeds and in certain types of vegetables.

Saturated or animal-based fats contribute to a building-up of cholesterol levels in the blood vessels, so polyunsaturated fats such as vegetable oils should be used for most purposes. Olive oil, for instance, is now strongly recommended as an essential part of the fat component of the daily diet as an anti-cholesterol agent. However, dairy products can be used in moderation.

**Carbohydrates** include sugars, starches and dietary fibre. Sugars, whether processed or 'natural', contribute little in a dietary sense apart from sweetness. Starches – present in vegetable and grain foods – are a cheap and healthy source of energy, and give lengthy satisfaction, but only so long as they are not heavily refined, when they lose much of their vitamin and dietary fibre content. This latter is the cellulose forming the main structure of grains, vegetables and fruit, plus the skin, peel and husk, which the body cannot digest; it does not contribute a significant amount of energy, but its dietary and health value lies in the fact that, because it is indigestible, it passes through the body quickly, helping to remove many other waste products. *Whole* products are best for health and for their fibre content.

**Vitamins, minerals and trace elements** are contained in most foods. In the absence of meat in the diet, so long as other valuable foods are being eaten – grains, pulses, dairy produce, fish, fresh vegetables and fruit – there is little danger of a deficiency.

Vitamins, however, can be lost by soaking and over-cooking, which highlights the value of eating foods in their most natural form. The sweet pepper eaten raw, for instance, retains and offers its full complement of Vitamin C and minerals, and thus raw vegetable and fruit salads are one of the main nutritive armaments of a meat-free diet. However, when carefully cooked, that same pepper will still have a wonderful flavour, and can still contribute a proportion of its original nutrients.

Choosing the best ingredients and cooking them carefully, thinking always about health, has been basic to my culinary and dietary philosophy for years. My 'Cuisine Naturelle' was based on the precepts of cooking delicious food without many of the ingredients which are thought to be deleterious to health. In general, the same ideas are relevant here.

# SOUPS AND GARNISHES

Soups of one sort or another – be they thick, virtually one-pot meals, or more sophisticated and delicate bowls of sheer flavour – are the mainstay of cuisines the world over. European cuisines in particular are rich in soups, dishes that are more representative of local cooking than any other. For nothing could be simpler than to sear a few seasonal local vegetables in fat of some kind, then add water or stock and a few flavourings, and to cook until ready to be eaten as is, or to be puréed to a smoother texture.

Nowadays soups in the West are often looked upon as the first course of a meal, but in many more culinary traditions soup is an essential for daily survival – think of the *harira* soups of Morocco, eaten at sundown after the day's fasting during Ramadan, and the *soupe aux oignons* which kept the market porters (and tourists) going at Les Halles in Paris. A soup and accompanying carbohydrate – whether in the form of bread, croûtons, pasta (in Italy) or dumplings (in the Balkan countries) – is often nourishing and sustaining enough to serve as the whole meal. This was certainly the case with the vegetable soup and potato dumplings which Chef Belá Liscsinszky, of the Golden Dragon restaurant, Szentendre, near Budapest, demonstrated to me; it utilised fresh local vegetables, soured cream and paprika.

Thick vegetable and pulse soups are staples of winter cuisine throughout Europe – the *garbures* of northern France, Scotch broth in Scotland, the cream soups of Britain and France, the lentil soups of Cyprus and Spain, and the various *zuppe* of Italy. If available, of course, meat was added, but usually the soups had a vegetable base, except in coastal areas, along rivers or beside freshwater lakes where fish could become part of the dish – the *bouillabaisse* and *bourrides* of France, the *waterzooie* of Belgium, the *zuppe de pesce* and

*Black bean soup with Spicy cornbread (see page 45)*

*sopas de pescados* of Italy and Spain respectively; in this tradition too was the Hungarian fisherman's soup, demonstrated to me by János Szôke Sipos, made with carp from the Danube.

Soups are associated with summer too, and can cool as well as heat. The famous Russian *borscht*, made with beetroots, is served cold, as are the fruit soups of the European continent – I encountered a delicious one made from sour cherries in Hungary. A variation on the Spanish *gazpacho*, perhaps the most internationally renowned of cold soups, is reproduced here.

I hope the brief selection in the following pages will demonstrate to some extent the wealth of flavours, textures and ingredients which soups, those most international of dishes, can offer.

# BLACK BEAN SOUP

### SERVES 4–6

| | |
|---|---|
| **200 g (7 oz) dried black beans, soaked in water overnight** | Drain, rinse and drain again. The beans should be fairly dry. |
| **45 ml (3 tablespoons) olive oil**<br>**1 onion, peeled and finely chopped**<br>**1 garlic clove, peeled and crushed** | Sweat together in a large saucepan for a few minutes. Add the black beans, and stir. |
| **2 litres (3½ pints) vegetable stock (see page 24)** | Add to the saucepan, and bring to the boil. Reduce heat to a simmer. |
| **1 celery stalk, trimmed and sliced**<br>**1 large carrot, peeled and cut into large chunks**<br>**2 sprigs of thyme**<br>**2 bay leaves**<br>**a pinch each of ground cloves and ground mace** | Add, and cook for approximately 1¼–1½ hours until the beans are soft.<br>Cool the mixture slightly. Remove the herbs, place the mixture in a food processor and blend until smooth. Return the mixture to the saucepan to reheat. |
| **salt and freshly ground pepper**<br>**60 ml (4 tablespoons) soured cream (optional)**<br>**2 chilli peppers, seeded and cut into fine dice**<br>**15 ml (1 tablespoon) finely cut coriander** | Correct seasoning with salt and pepper, then serve in warm bowls with a spoonful of soured cream (if used), and a sprinkle each of chopped chilli and coriander. |

 These beans, which belong to the kidney bean family, are shiny, very black, and have a full, meaty flavour. They are very popular in the Caribbean and the southern United States. (They are *not* the same beans as those fermented for use in Chinese and Japanese cooking.)

# LENTIL SOUP

**SERVES 4–6**

| | |
|---|---|
| **200 g (7 oz) red lentils** | Wash and drain. |
| **1 onion, peeled and finely chopped**<br>**45 ml (3 tablespoons) olive oil**<br>**1 garlic clove, peeled and crushed**<br>**15 g (½ oz) fresh ginger, peeled and grated** | Place in a large saucepan and sweat together, about 5 minutes. |
| **1 carrot, peeled and finely chopped**<br>**1 celery stalk, trimmed and finely chopped**<br>**2.5 ml (½ teaspoon) each of cumin seeds, and ground coriander**<br>**1.2 litres (2 pints) vegetable stock (see page 24)** | Add to the pan along with the lentils, and bring to the boil. |
| **1 sprig of thyme**<br>**1 bay leaf** | Add, and simmer, covered, for approximately 25 minutes. Allow the mixture to cool slightly, and remove the herbs.<br>Place the mixture into a food processor and blend until smooth. |
| **salt and freshly ground pepper**<br>**croûtons (see page 25) and**<br>**30 ml (2 tablespoons) cut chives to garnish** | Return the soup to the pan, season to taste with salt and pepper, and correct the consistency if desired with extra stock. Serve garnished with croûtons and chives. |

The soup can be rough or smooth textured. For a smoother soup, sieve after blending.
Other types of lentils may be used instead.

# FISH SOUP WITH LEEK AND SPINACH

**SERVES 4**

| | |
|---|---|
| **300 g (11 oz) fish fillets (salmon, halibut or mackerel)**<br>**1 medium leek, washed**<br>**1.5 cm (¾ in) knob of fresh ginger, peeled** | Cut the fish into very fine slices, cut the leek into fine rings, and cut the ginger into fine strips. |
| **15 ml (1 tablespoon) olive oil** | Heat in a small frying pan, and stir-fry the ginger and leek for 2–3 minutes. Remove from the heat and drain. |
| **100 g (4 oz) young spinach leaves, washed and picked** | Place in the bottom of a soup tureen or individual serving bowls. Add the leek and ginger and arrange the slices of fish on top. |
| **salt and freshly ground pepper**<br>**45 ml (3 tablespoons) finely cut spring onions**<br>**30 ml (2 tablespoons) picked chervil** | Season with a little salt and pepper, and sprinkle with the spring onion and chervil. |
| **800 ml (scant 1½ pints) good flavoured fish or vegetable stock (see page 24)** | Bring to the boil, pour over the fish and other ingredients, and serve immediately. |

Cut the fish into very fine strips so that the boiling stock cooks it immediately.

*Fish soup with leek and spinach*

# Pumpkin Soup with Cheese Croûtons

**SERVES 8**

| | |
|---|---|
| 30 ml (2 tablespoons) olive oil<br>1 onion, peeled and finely sliced | Sweat together in a large saucepan until the onion is soft. |
| 1 kg (2¼ lb) pumpkin flesh, cut into chunks<br>finely grated zest and juice of 1 orange<br>powdered cinnamon<br>salt and freshly ground pepper | Add, seasoning to taste with a pinch of cinnamon, salt and pepper.<br>Cover with a lid, and let cook gently for 10 minutes. |
| 2 litres (3½ pints) vegetable stock (see page 24) | Add about three-quarters of the stock, and simmer for another 15 minutes until the pumpkin is soft and tender. Pour the mixture into a blender or food mill. Blend until smooth and return the soup to the pot. |
| 100 ml (3½ fl oz) single cream<br>freshly grated nutmeg | Add, along with more stock if necessary to thin, then correct the seasoning, adding a little nutmeg. Keep hot. |
| 30 g (1¼ oz) butter<br>15 ml (1 tablespoon) olive oil<br>200 g (7 oz) stale bread, cubed | Melt butter and oil together and fry the bread cubes until golden brown. |
| 150 g (5 oz) Appenzell cheese, grated | Sprinkle on top of the croûtons. |
| 50 ml (2 fl oz) single cream | Add, and turn the croûtons so they are covered in cream and cheese. Pour soup into hot bowls, and divide the croûtons between the bowls. |
| 30 ml (2 tablespoons) snipped chives | Sprinkle over the soup, and serve. |

# Seasonal Vegetable Soup

**SERVES 4–6**

1 small onion, peeled
  and diced
100 g (4 oz) carrots,
  scrubbed and sliced
100 g (4 oz) celeriac,
  peeled and cut into
  slices approx. 2.5 cm
  (1 in) square
100 g (4 oz) leek,
  trimmed and sliced
4 sprigs of thyme
30 ml (2 tablespoons)
  olive oil
salt and pepper

Sweat together for a few minutes, then season lightly.

---

2 litres (3½ pints)
  vegetable stock (see
  page 24)
100 g (4 oz) each of
  haricot and flageolet
  beans, cooked

Add half the stock, plus the beans, turn to mix, then
bring to the boil.

---

100 g (4 oz) pumpkin
  flesh, cut into 1 cm
  (½ in) cubes
100 g (4 oz) kohlrabi,
  peeled, cut into 8 and
  finely sliced
100 g (4 oz) courgettes,
  trimmed and cut into
  thin rounds
100 g (4 oz) cabbage,
  finely shredded

Add the pumpkin and kohlrabi and cook for 5
minutes before adding the rest of the vegetables.
Add more stock as you go along.
Simmer until everything is tender but still retains a
little texture (about 15–20 minutes).

---

30 ml (2 tablespoons)
  finely chopped
  parsley
garlic croûtons (see
  page 25)

Garnish with parsley, and serve with garlic croûtons.

---

This is an autumn selection of vegetables. Choose from what is
best per season.

# POTATO DUMPLINGS

### SERVES 4–6

**250 g (9 oz) potatoes, cooked, peeled and mashed**
**1 egg**
**50 g (2 oz) plain flour**
**salt**
**freshly grated nutmeg**

Mix together, seasoning to taste with salt and nutmeg.
Form into walnut-sized dumplings and cook, a few at a time, in boiling salted water until the dumplings rise to the surface.
Remove using a slotted spoon and put into boiling soup. Serve immediately.

 These dumplings, the recipe for which was given to me by Béla Liscsinszky, of the Golden Dragon Restaurant at Szentendre, would be good added to any thick vegetable soup.

# CREAM OF ONION SOUP

### SERVES 4–6

**500 g (18 oz) onions, peeled and finely sliced**
**50 g (2 oz) unsalted butter**

Sweat together over a low heat, stirring occasionally, until softened.

**100 ml (3½ fl oz) dry white wine**

Add, and continue cooking until the liquid has almost disappeared.

**1 litre (1¾ pints) vegetable stock (see page 24)**

Add, bring to the boil, cover and simmer for about 30 minutes.

**100 ml (3½ fl oz) double cream**

Add, cook for another 5 minutes. Cool a little, then purée in a liquidiser or blender.

**salt and freshly ground pepper**
**50 ml (2 fl oz) double cream, whipped**

Season to taste with salt and pepper, and add the whipped cream just before serving so you get a lovely froth on the top.

# UDON POT

**SERVES 4**

**4 large Chinese cabbage leaves**
**200 g (7 oz) *daikon* radish**
**200 g (7 oz) young leek**
**100 g (4 oz) spinach or chrysanthemum leaves**
**8 *shiitake* mushrooms**
**150 g (5 oz) *tofu***

Blanch, refresh and cut the cabbage leaves into 7.5 cm (3 in) lengths. Peel the radish, cut into 1 cm (½ in) rounds and blanch. Cut the leek into 1 cm (½ in) rounds, wash and blanch. Trim the spinach leaves and wash. Wash and drain the mushrooms. Cut the *tofu* into 2 cm (¾ in) cubes.

---

**75 g (3 oz) squid**
**120 g (4½ oz) each of salmon and mackerel fillet**

Cut each into four pieces.

---

**200–300 g (7–11 oz) dried *udon* noodles**

Cook in plenty of water to *al dente*, about 12–15 minutes. Refresh in cold water and drain.

---

**1 litre (1¾ pints) fish stock (see page 24)**
**30 ml (2 tablespoons) each of soy sauce and *saké***

Bring to the boil together.
Place the noodles in the bottom of a casserole.
Arrange the vegetables, *tofu* and seafood on top. Pour in the boiling stock and simmer until the noodles are warmed and the seafood is cooked.

---

**5 ml (1 teaspoon) grated fresh ginger**
**30 ml (2 tablespoons) chopped spring onion**
**a pinch of 7-flavour spice (*shichimi-togarashi*)**

Sprinkle over the dish and serve.

---

This dish may be prepared in one large or four individual casseroles.
It can be cooked at the table in a deep electric skillet or a casserole set on a table-top gas cooker. Bring the stock to a simmer in the pot and have the vegetables, *tofu* and noodles ready prepared and blanched on a platter. The guests can cook for themselves, starting with the seafood and vegetables; the noodles are added at the end and eaten with the stock when it has become most flavourful.
The stock can also be flavoured with red *miso*.

# Yellow Tomato Gazpacho

**SERVES 4**

1 kg (2¼ lb) ripe yellow tomatoes, seeded and coarsely chopped
½ cucumber, peeled, seeded and coarsely chopped
2 yellow peppers, cored, seeded and coarsely chopped
2 garlic cloves, peeled and crushed
1 small onion, peeled and coarsely chopped
6 basil leaves
approx. 30 ml (2 tablespoons) white wine vinegar
100 ml (3½ fl oz) olive oil
salt and freshly ground pepper

Mix together in a large bowl, seasoning to taste with salt and pepper. Cover and leave to marinate overnight in a cool place.

---

300 ml (10 fl oz) vegetable stock (see page 24)

Add, then pour the vegetables and liquid in small batches into the food processor and blend until smooth. Place in a bowl and chill.

---

sugar, lemon juice and Tabasco sauce

Correct the seasoning just before serving.

---

60 ml (4 tablespoons) Mascarpone cheese
60 ml (4 tablespoons) finely diced red pepper
4 sprigs of basil

Serve in chilled soup cups or bowls, garnishing each with a spoonful of Mascarpone, a sprinkle of red pepper dice and a sprig of basil.

---

*Yellow tomato gazpacho with Parmesan, spring onion and coriander puffs (see page 44)*

# Vegetable Stock

**MAKES ABOUT 1 LITRE (1¾ PINTS)**

| | |
|---|---|
| **40 g (1½ oz) each of onion and leek**<br>**20 g (¾ oz) each of celery and fennel**<br>**30 g (1¼ oz) each of cabbage and tomato** | Peel, trim, wash, etc as appropriate, cut up and chop finely. Keep them separate. |
| **30 ml (2 tablespoons) vegetable oil** | Heat in a large pan and sweat the onion and leek in it for 4–5 minutes.<br>Add the remaining vegetables and sweat for a further 10 minutes. |
| **1.2 litres (2 pints) water**<br>**½ bay leaf**<br>**1 small clove**<br>**salt and freshly ground pepper** | Add, and simmer for 20 minutes.<br>Strain through a fine sieve or cloth, allowing it to drip.<br>Season to taste with salt and pepper.<br>Use immediately, or refrigerate for a short time, or freeze in small containers. |

This is the stock to use for vegetarian soups and other dishes. It can also be used, reduced, in sauces like tomato, and in salad dressings instead of olive or other oil.

# Fish Stock

**MAKES ABOUT 1 LITRE (1¾ PINTS)**

| | |
|---|---|
| **900 g (2 lb) white fish bones and trimmings** | Wash thoroughly, and chop up finely. |
| **30 ml (2 tablespoons) vegetable oil**<br>**60 g (2½ oz) mixed onion, white of leek, celeriac, fennel leaves and dill, finely chopped**<br>**30 g (1¼ oz) mushroom trimmings** | Sweat together in a suitable pan until the vegetables have softened. |

| | |
|---|---|
| **1.2 litres (2 pints) water**<br>**60 ml (4 tablespoons)**<br>**white wine** | Add, along with the fish bones and trimmings, and simmer for 20 minutes, occasionally skimming and removing any fat.<br>Strain through a cloth or fine sieve. |
| **salt and freshly ground**<br>**pepper** | Season to taste with salt and pepper.<br>Use immediately, keep in the refrigerator for a short time, or freeze in small containers. |

 This stock is the one to use in fish soups and all other fish dishes.

# GARLIC CROÛTONS

**SERVES 4**

| | |
|---|---|
| **1 large garlic clove,**<br>**peeled and bruised**<br>**60 ml (4 tablespoons)**<br>**clarified butter (see**<br>**below)** OR OLIVE OIL | Rub a small frying pan with the garlic, then cook it in the butter over a low heat until just beginning to colour. Remove the garlic from the pan. |
| **2 slices of bread, cut**<br>**into 5 mm (¼ in)**<br>**cubes** | Add, and cook evenly until golden brown in colour. |
| **salt and freshly ground**<br>**pepper** | Drain the croûtons on kitchen paper and lightly season. |

 Clarified butter can be cooked to a higher temperature and keeps for a long time without refrigeration (all the milk solids having been removed). Heat butter until it melts, at a very low heat, then wait until all the impurities sink to the bottom, still on the heat. Cool slightly, then put through muslin into an airtight jar.

# BREADS AND SAVOURY BAKING

When primitive man domesticated grains, he became civilised man. From those grains came flour, and when those flours were mixed with water, basic bread was formed. Bread of some sort or another is a staple of most cuisines throughout the world, from the unleavened (or unraised) *chapattis* of India and *tortillas* of Mexico, to the yeasted (or raised) breads of Europe.

The grains used vary. Wheat is one of the commonest because it contains the most gluten, and gluten, formed when wheat flour proteins are mixed with water, helps bread doughs to rise. However, in many countries in Europe where wheat was not a predominant crop, other breads developed; most of these were coarser and heavier because the grains used – barley, buckwheat, millet or rye – contained little or no gluten.

The flours used in any bread to be part of a natural, meat-free diet, must be whole and unrefined. Try to use organic stone-ground wholewheat flour, for instance, as this process involves less heat, and means fewer nutrients are destroyed. (Interestingly, the yeast used in leavened breads is an excellent source of a wide range of vitamins, particularly B1 and B2.) And try to *mix* flours as I have done in many of the following recipes; the health, flavour and texture benefits are enormous.

Breads and other savoury baked foods are not just served *with* foods, they are crumbed for toppings and coatings, used in dumplings, in desserts, and sliced as the *base* for foods. This latter practice probably dates from medieval times when lords and ladies would distribute their meat-juice-soaked platters of dried bread to the poor. This basic concept, of bread as edible plate, is most familiar to us in the famous Danish open sandwich or smørrebrød (literally buttered bread). Even canapés, the finger-sized foods eaten at drinks parties, are related to this idea.

*Crabmeat samosas (see page 67), savoury scones
and bread rolls with a variety of fillings*

The concept probably reaches its height in the Italian bread dough 'platter' known as pizza; this was invented by the Neapolitans, and has since been considerably adapted. The one I baked for Peto at the Pizzeria Castello in London had a wholemeal base.

That basic flour and water mixture also forms pastry, and the combination of pastry and filling or topping continues the edible plate theme – the *quiches* of Lorraine, the patties and pies of Britain, the *coulibiac* of Russia, the *filo*-wrapped packages of Turkey and Greece, and the savoury and sweet *strudels* of the Balkan countries. Even scones and muffins, pancakes, *crêpes* and the incomparable *blinis* – all to bear or enclose toppings or fillings – are extensions of the basic idea, as is the batter which forms the outer casing of foods to be deep-fried. Flour and water are magic indeed.

# RYE BREAD

**MAKES 2 LOAVES**

**OVEN:** Moderately hot, 200°C/400°F/Gas 6

| | |
|---|---|
| 300 g (11 oz) rye flour<br>300 g (11 oz) white<br>  flour<br>5 ml (1 teaspoon) salt | Stir together in a bowl, and make a well in the middle. |
| 25 g (1 oz) fresh yeast<br>5 ml (1 teaspoon) sugar | Cream together to a liquid. |
| 300 ml (10 fl oz) milk<br>  and water mixed,<br>  warmed to blood<br>  temperature | Add to the yeast mixture and mix well. |
| 15 ml (1 tablespoon)<br>  black treacle | Add to the well in the dry ingredients along with the yeast mixture, and mix in gradually to make a firm dough. Knead well on a lightly floured surface. Cover with a cloth and leave in a warm place to prove for 1½ hours.<br>Knock the dough down and shape into two round loaves. Place on a baking sheet.<br>Cover with a cloth and leave to prove again for 45 minutes in a warm place.<br>Bake in the preheated oven for 35–40 minutes. Remove from the oven and leave to cool. |

You could make one round loaf, and use the remaining dough to make tiny loaves in tins of 11 × 6 cm (4¼ × 2½ in).
Rye bread is popular in Scandinavia and the USSR. It contains little gluten, so is dense, but it has great flavour.
In this and the other yeast–raised bread recipes, you can use half quantity dried yeast. Follow instructions on the packet.

# Millet Granary Bread

**MAKES 1 LOAF**

**OVEN:** Moderately hot, 200°C/400°F/Gas 6, then cool, 150°C/300°F/Gas 2

| | |
|---|---|
| **100 g (4 oz) millet**<br>**100 ml (3½ fl oz) water** | Place in a saucepan and bring just to the boil. Cool and drain. |
| **25 g (1 oz) fresh yeast**<br>**250 ml (8 fl oz)<br>  lukewarm water**<br>**15 ml (1 tablespoon)<br>  honey** | Mix together to dissolve. |
| **300 g (11 oz) wholemeal<br>  flour**<br>**75 g (3 oz) rye flour**<br>**75 g (3 oz) oatmeal**<br>**50 g (2 oz) wheat or rye<br>  flakes**<br>**5 ml (1 teaspoon) salt** | Place with the millet into the bowl of an electric mixer fitted with the dough hook. Add the yeast mixture and mix in, using the hook, until the dough leaves the sides of the bowl.<br>Turn out on to a lightly floured board, and knead into a ball. Place in a floured bowl, cover with a cloth and leave to rise for approximately 1 hour in a warm place until doubled in size.<br>Turn out again, and knock the dough back. Shape into a round, and place on a baking sheet. Leave to prove again for about 30 minutes.<br>Brush with cold water. Score the top and bake in the preheated oven on preheated quarry tiles or a pizza stone for about 45–60 minutes. Reduce the temperature after 20 minutes' baking. |

Breads baked on quarry tiles or pizza stones have a special crustiness to them. The tile or stone absorbs moisture from the baking loaves and this crisps the bottom crust.
The tiles or stone need a minimum of 45 minutes' preheating.
Millet has as high a protein content as wheat.

# OPEN SANDWICHES

Herbed cream cheese with tomato and finely sliced red onion on *pumpernickel* bread.

Stilton and cream cheese mixed together with finely chopped celery on wholegrain bread, garnished with celery leaves and cress.

Small muffins, cut in half, toasted and topped with avocado slices, seasoned with salt, pepper, chives, lemon juice and oil and topped with a fried quail's egg.

Classic Blinis (buckwheat pancakes, see page 116): topped with smoked salmon, soured cream and caviar.

Mini pitta breads, stuffed with:
– *hummus* (see page 109), roasted peppers (see page 97), Feta cheese and olives.
– fresh spinach and Stilton or other blue cheese cut into 'vermicelli' on a grater.

Marinated kipper with slices of apple and onion on granary bread.

Avocado slices with marinated salmon in orange and dill dressing garnished with wheat sprouts, on black rye bread.

Feta cheese with grilled vegetables (courgettes, aubergines, peppers) on onion bagels.

---

The kings of the open sandwiches are the Danes, whose *smørrebrød* (meaning simply buttered bread) is famous the world over.
Serve as a satisfying snack or as a lunch.
Small rolls, scones or sandwiches, with a variety of fillings rather than toppings, can be served at afternoon tea. See page 27 for a few more ideas.

*A few open sandwich ideas, along with some of the cheese canapés on page 162*

# ZOPF

**MAKES 1 PLAITED LOAF**

**OVEN:** Moderately hot, 190°C/375°F/Gas 5

| | |
|---|---|
| 15 g (½ oz) fresh yeast<br>5 ml (1 teaspoon) honey<br>250 ml (8 fl oz)<br>  lukewarm milk | Cream the yeast and honey together in about 30 ml (2 tablespoons) of the warm milk. |
| 50 g (2 oz) butter,<br>  melted<br>5 ml (1 teaspoon) salt | Add along with the rest of the milk to the yeast mixture. |
| 450 g (1 lb) strong<br>  white flour | Place in a bowl, and make a well in the centre. Gradually mix in the yeast mixture. |
| 1 egg, beaten | Add, and mix in well, then knead well for about 5 minutes on a lightly floured surface.<br>Cover with a cloth and leave to rise in a warm place for about 1½ hours.<br>Knock back the dough and divide into three equal pieces. Shape each piece into a long thin strip. Start to plait together from the centre. Turn the loaf around and plait from the other end.<br>Cover with a cloth and set to rise a second time for about 30 minutes. Before baking, put in a cool place for 10 minutes. |
| 1 egg yolk | Brush over the bread and bake in the preheated oven for 45 minutes. Leave to cool. |

This is the traditional Swiss Sunday loaf, similar to the Jewish *chollah*, but plaited differently. You could also divide the dough into two long strips, bend these in half together and plait *four* strips.
I like to make finger-sized zopf for afternoon tea sandwiches. Milk instead of water makes a softer bread.

# BREAD ROLLS

## MAKES ABOUT 40–50 ROLLS

**OVEN:** Very hot, 240°C/475°F/Gas 9

| | |
|---|---|
| 50 g (2 oz) fresh yeast<br>15 ml (1 tablespoon)<br>  honey<br>500 ml (18 fl oz)<br>  lukewarm water | Cream together, using 50 ml (2 fl oz) of the water. |
| 1 kg (2¼ lb) strong<br>  white flour<br>10 ml (2 teaspoons) salt | Place in a bowl, and make a well in the centre. Add the yeast mixture and remaining water and mix in to make a pliable dough. Knead well on a lightly floured surface, and shape into a ball. Place in a clean bowl, lightly dust with extra flour. Cover with a cloth and leave to rise for 45–60 minutes in a warm place.<br>Knock the dough back and shape into rolls. Place on a greased baking tray. |
| poppy or sesame seeds | Sprinkle over the rolls, then cover with a cloth and leave to prove for another 15–20 minutes.<br>Bake in the preheated oven for approximately 15 minutes until golden brown. Cool. |

The basic dough can be flavoured with spinach or tomato purées, with herbs, or chopped sautéed onions. Divide the dough into three or four, and mix in about 30 ml (2 tablespoons) – or to taste – of the chosen flavouring.

Make tiny rolls, or normal-sized ones, using about 25–50 g (1–2 oz) dough per roll. I like to serve tiny filled rolls for afternoon tea.

Shape as you please – in rounds, oblongs, twists, plaits, or simply rounds with a cross snipped in the top with scissors. Any rolls you do not need immediately freeze well.

# LEEK AND ONION SCONES

**MAKES ABOUT 15 SCONES**

**OVEN: Moderately hot, 200°C/400°F/Gas 6**

| | |
|---|---|
| 100 g (4 oz) onions, peeled and chopped<br>50 g (2 oz) leek, trimmed and cut into fine rings<br>15 ml (1 tablespoon) olive oil<br>salt and freshly ground pepper | Sweat together for a few minutes, then season to taste with salt and pepper. |
| 150 g (5 oz) wholewheat flour<br>100 g (4 oz) rye flour<br>10 ml (2 teaspoons) baking powder | Place in a large mixing bowl along with 2.5 ml (½ teaspoon) salt. |
| 30 g (1¼ oz) butter | Rub into the flours. |
| 15 ml (1 tablespoon) chopped fresh thyme (optional)<br>150 ml (5 fl oz) buttermilk or milk | Mix in along with the onion mixture, until a medium soft dough.<br>Turn out on to a floured board and pat to approximately 2 cm (¾ in) thick. Cut with a 4–5 cm (1½–2 in) round cutter, and place on a baking sheet. Dust the scones with extra flour and bake in the preheated oven for about 15 minutes. |

Grated cheese can be added to the mixture.
Serve with soups or stews instead of bread. They're good at tea too.
I like to serve these as a savoury scone with smoked fish and horseradish cream, or with cream cheese and chives.

# POPOVERS

**MAKES 24**

**OVEN:** Moderately hot, 200°C/400°F/Gas 6

| | |
|---|---|
| **120 g (4½ oz) plain flour**<br>**250 ml (8 fl oz) milk** | In a large bowl, whisk together. |
| **50 g (2 oz) unsalted butter, melted**<br>**2 large eggs, beaten** | Beat in until smooth and the consistency of single cream. |
| **salt and freshly ground pepper**<br>**15 ml (1 tablespoon) roughly chopped fresh sage** | Stir in, seasoning to taste.<br>Let the mixture stand and rest for approximately 1 hour. |
| **about 25–50 g (1–2 oz) vegetable fat or oil** | Grease 24 patty pans with a little fat or oil, and place in the preheated oven. When the fat is hot, ladle the batter in to half fill the pans, and bake for approximately 20–30 minutes until the popovers are golden brown and crisp. (If not baked enough, they will collapse when removed from the pan.) |

To make cheese popovers, add 50 g (2 oz) grated Gruyère cheese to the batter before baking.
You could also add a small croûton or two to the patty pans before adding the batter. This provides an interesting and unexpected texture.
The popovers could form the container or base for a vegetable stew.

# BASIC PIZZA DOUGH

**MAKES 2 DEEP OR 4 LARGE PIZZA BASES
OR 6 CALZONE**

**OVEN:** Moderately hot, 200°C/400°F/Gas 6

15 g (½ oz) fresh yeast
150 ml (5 fl oz) warm
  water
10 ml (2 teaspoons)
  honey

Dissolve the yeast in the warm water with the honey.
Set aside in a warm place until the mixture starts to
bubble (about 7–10 minutes).

200 g (7 oz) white bread
  flour
100 g (4 oz) wholemeal
  or rye flour
5 ml (1 teaspoon) salt
60 ml (4 tablespoons)
  olive oil

Combine the flours, salt and 45 ml (3 tablespoons) of
the olive oil in a mixing bowl. Add the yeast mixture.
Stir until the ingredients come together roughly.
Turn the dough on to a lightly floured board and
knead until smooth, adding more flour as necessary.
Clean the bowl, brush it with the remaining olive oil
and return the kneaded dough to the bowl. Turn the
dough over so the whole surface is covered with the
oil. Cover and let the dough rise in a warm place
until doubled in size (about 30 minutes).
Turn the dough out on to a floured board, knead,
then leave to rest for another 15 minutes.
Divide the dough into two or four, and shape into
flat circles. You can simply roll them to 20 cm (8 in)
flat rounds, or do it the proper way, as follows.
Starting from the centre work the dough with your
fingertips, pressing down firmly and quickly in a
circular motion, working from the inside out.
Lift the dough from the work surface and drape it
over your fist. Hold your hands together and move
them apart, stretching the dough over them as you
do, until the dough is the right size. Always stretch
the dough close to the thicker outer edge as the
centre becomes thinner.
Place the pizza base in an oiled pan (or on an oiled
baking sheet), and brush the base with some extra
virgin olive oil. It is now ready to be filled.
Bake in the preheated oven, about 7–8 minutes.

An assortment of herbs and flavourings can be added to the
basic pizza dough. And you could, for instance, make it into
breadsticks with fennel seeds.

*A smoked salmon, soured cream and dill pizza*

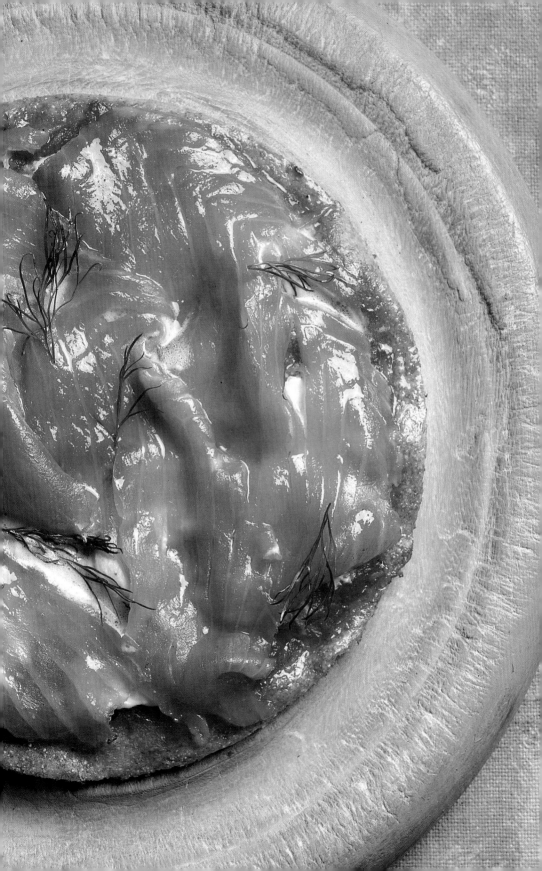

# A Dozen Pizza
# Topping Suggestions

Always brush the pizza base with some extra virgin olive oil before filling and baking.

**1** Spread with slices of Mozzarella and goat's cheese with tomato sauce (opposite) or roughly chopped sun-dried tomatoes in oil topped with finely sliced red onion. Sprinkle with fresh chopped thyme and bake. Brush with more extra virgin olive oil, and sprinkle on some fresh herbs and grated Parmesan cheese before serving.

**2** Spread with a thin layer of tomato *concassée* (opposite) and finely sliced onion. Bake. Garnish with finely sliced smoked salmon, soured cream and dill, and flash in the oven for a minute. Add some caviar if you feel extravagant.

**3** Spread with slices of Mozzarella and grated Fontina cheese (this is the basic cheese mixture), and top with sun-dried tomato pieces and king prawns (which have been peeled and cut in halves lengthwise). Sprinkle with lots of basil and bake.

**4** Spread with tomato purée, grated Fontina, sautéed leek rings and chopped onion or shallot, a little tomato *concassée*, and top with cooked mussels and sliced Mozzarella. Bake.

**5** Spread with sautéed sliced new potatoes, black olives, cherry tomato halves and tomato paste. Bake.

**6** Spread with the basic cheese mixture (see 3 above), with the addition of some roasted red pepper sauce (see page 97). Garnish with strips of sweet pepper, and bake.

**7** Spread with your favourite mixture of vegetables stir-fried in sesame oil with chopped garlic and ginger for a couple of minutes. Top with some cherry tomato halves, pine nuts, finely chopped spring onion and fresh coriander. Bake.

**8** Spread with *tapenade* (opposite), followed by layers of the basic cheese mixture (see 3 above). Garnish with diced tomato, finely sliced shallot rings, and a sprinkling of herbs and olive oil. Bake.

**9** Spread with Mozzarella slices and tomato sauce (opposite), and top with pre-cooked aubergine. Sprinkle with fresh chopped oregano and bake. Drizzle with *pesto* (see page 89) and grated Parmesan cheese before serving.

**10** Spread with Mozzarella slices and tomato sauce (opposite), top with sautéed courgette slices, and chunks of goat cheese. Sprinkle with thyme and garlic oil (see page 137), then bake.

**11** Spread with sautéed artichoke bottoms and fennel, with cherry tomato halves and chunks of goat cheese. Bake.

**12** Spread with sautéed leek circles, *trompette* mushrooms, smoked haddock mixed with a little cream, and bake. Break some quails eggs on top a few minutes before the end of cooking time.

# TOMATO SAUCE

30 ml (2 tablespoons)
  olive oil
1 small onion, peeled
2 garlic cloves, peeled
10 coriander seeds,
  crushed

Finely chop onion and garlic. Heat all together in a large saucepan, and cook gently until the onions are soft.

1 kg (2¼ lb) ripe red
  tomatoes, skinned,
  seeded and chopped
15 ml (1 tablespoon)
  tomato purée
4 basil leaves
5 ml (1 teaspoon)
  chopped oregano
salt, freshly ground
  pepper and sugar

Add, and season with salt, pepper and sugar.
Stir to mix in the seasoning, then bring to a simmer.
Cook uncovered, stirring from time to time, until most of the liquid has evaporated (about 20 minutes).

Tomato *concassée* is useful in many recipes. Nick the skin of each tomato, immerse in boiling water for 10 seconds and then remove. Peel off the skin and halve the tomato. Remove the seeds using a teaspoon, then chop the flesh very finely.

# TAPENADE

250 g (9 oz) oil-cured
  black olives, pitted
1 garlic clove, peeled
22.5 ml (1½
  tablespoons) capers,
  drained
50 g (2 oz) anchovy
  fillets, drained
60 ml (4 tablespoons)
  olive oil
juice of 1 lemon

Combine all the ingredients in a blender and blend until a smooth sauce is formed.
Store in the refrigerator.

This is a very versatile mixture which comes from the south of France. It can also be used as a dip, or spread on bread canapé bases. The flavour goes particularly well with hard-boiled eggs as a canapé.

# ONION CALZONE

**MAKES 6**

**OVEN: Hot, 230°C/450°F/Gas 8**

| | |
|---|---|
| 1 quantity Basic Pizza Dough (see page 36) | Divide into six pieces, and roll each piece out to a circle 20 cm (8 in) in diameter. |
| 45 ml (3 tablespoons) olive oil<br>900 g (2 lb) onions, peeled and finely sliced<br>5 ml (1 teaspoon) fresh chopped oregano | Heat together and cook until the onion is soft but not brown. |
| 100 g (4 oz) Mozzarella cheese, diced<br>25 g (1 oz) Pecorino cheese, grated<br>salt and pepper | Mix into the onions, and season with salt and pepper. Spread the filling evenly on to the lower half of each pizza dough circle. |
| 1 egg yolk | Brush over the edges of the dough circles, fold these over and crimp the edges securely together. Transfer each *calzone*, using a spatula, to a well greased baking sheet, and brush the tops with the remaining egg. Bake in the preheated oven for 20 minutes until the tops are golden. |

# CHEESE CALZONE

| | |
|---|---|
| 350 g (12 oz) Ricotta cheese<br>1 egg<br>225 g (8 oz) Mozzarella cheese, diced<br>50 g (2 oz) Parmesan cheese, grated<br>salt and pepper<br>freshly grated nutmeg | Mix together, and use as the filling for six pizza dough *calzone* as above. |

# Leek and Goat Cheese Flan

**MAKES 1 FLAN**

**OVEN:** Moderately hot, 200°C/400°F/Gas 6, then moderate, 180°C/350°C/Gas 4

| | |
|---|---|
| 1 blind-baked flan case (see next recipe) | Make up the bread-pastry dough, roll and blind-bake as described overleaf. Remove from the oven, and turn the oven down. |

| | |
|---|---|
| 25 g (1 oz) butter<br>15 ml (1 tablespoon) olive oil<br>450 g (1 lb) young leeks, washed, trimmed and thinly sliced | Sweat together in a large pan, and cook until the leek is soft, approximately 10 minutes. |

| | |
|---|---|
| 250 g (9 oz) *pyramide* goat cheese, crumbled<br>2 eggs<br>200 ml (7 fl oz) single cream<br>5 ml (1 teaspoon) chopped fresh thyme<br>salt and freshly ground pepper<br>cayenne pepper | Mix together in a bowl and season to taste with salt, pepper and cayenne.<br>Spread the leeks into the pastry case, and pour the cheese mixture evenly on top.<br>Bake in the preheated moderate oven for approximately 40 minutes until set and light golden in colour. |

# Carrot and Broad Bean Flan

**MAKES 1 FLAN**

**OVEN:** Moderately hot, 200°C/400°F/Gas 6, then 190°C/375°C/Gas 5

100 g (4 oz) each of rye and white flours
5 ml (1 teaspoon) powdered cumin
5 ml (1 teaspoon) salt
a pinch of pepper

Put all the dough ingredients into a mixer and mix together, or do by hand.
Mix together in a bowl, and make a well in the centre.

45 ml (3 tablespoons) vegetable oil
75 ml (5 tablespoons) natural yoghurt
1 small onion, peeled and finely chopped
1 garlic clove, peeled and finely chopped
1 egg yolk

Add to the well, mix together, then knead to a smooth dough. Make into a ball and allow to rest in the refrigerator for approximately 30 minutes.
Roll out and use to line a deep-sided 20 cm (8 in) flan tin. Cover with foil or greaseproof paper, and fill with baking beans. Bake in the preheated oven for 10 minutes.
Remove paper or foil and beans, and return to the oven for another 5 minutes until cooked.

150 g (5 oz) carrots, peeled and sliced
250 ml (8 fl oz) vegetable stock (see page 24)
1 sprig of thyme

Meanwhile, bring to the boil together in a saucepan, and cook for about 5 minutes. Drain and cool slightly.

175 g (6 oz) podded broad beans, blanched and skinned

Arrange on the bottom of the flan case, and arrange the carrot slices in overlapping circles on top.

120 ml (4 fl oz) milk
50 ml (2 fl oz) single cream
1 small onion, peeled and studded with 2 cloves (optional)

Heat together to just below boiling point.

2 large eggs, beaten

Place in a bowl, and add the heated milk and cream.

| salt and pepper<br>freshly grated nutmeg | Mix well, strain then correct seasoning with salt, pepper and nutmeg. Pour carefully into flan case. |
| --- | --- |
| 5 ml (1 teaspoon) dill<br>  or lemon thyme<br>  leaves, chopped | Scatter on the top of the flan, then bake in the oven at the reduced temperature for approximately 25 minutes until the custard has set. Serve warm. |

This savoury bread-pastry base can be used for a number of other flan fillings – or can be used as a pizza base.
Any leftover dough can be made into little biscuits. Glaze with egg wash and sprinkle with sesame seeds if you like.

# PARMESAN, SPRING ONION AND CORIANDER PUFFS

**MAKES 10**

**OVEN:** Moderately hot, 200°C/400°F/Gas 6

| 75 ml (2½ fl oz) water<br>75 ml (2½ fl oz) milk<br>a pinch of salt<br>50 g (2 oz) unsalted<br>  butter, cut into pieces | Bring to the boil together in a saucepan. |
| --- | --- |
| 75 g (3 oz) plain flour,<br>  sieved | Add, and beat the mixture with a wooden spoon. Cook until the mixture leaves the side of the pan and forms a ball (as for choux pastry). Remove from the heat and cool slightly. |
| 3 large eggs | Beat in, one at a time, then mix well. |
| 40 g (1½ oz) Parmesan<br>  cheese, finely grated<br>1 spring onion, finely<br>  chopped<br>15 ml (1 tablespoon)<br>  chopped coriander<br>freshly ground pepper<br>cayenne pepper | Stir in and season to taste with pepper and cayenne. Spoon the paste to form little rounds on a damp baking sheet. Bake in the preheated oven for approximately 25–30 minutes until the puffs are well puffed up, crisp and golden. |

# SPICY CORNBREAD WITH SUN-DRIED TOMATOES

**MAKES ABOUT 15–18**

**OVEN:** Moderately hot, 200°C/400°F/Gas 6

| | |
|---|---|
| fat for greasing | Grease the cornbread moulds (or Swiss roll tin, see below). |
| 100 g (4 oz) plain flour<br>100 g (4 oz) fine yellow cornmeal<br>15 ml (1 tablespoon) baking powder<br>5 ml (1 teaspoon) salt<br>7.5 ml (1½ teaspoons) caster sugar | Combine in a large bowl, and make a well in the centre. |
| 250 ml (8 fl oz) buttermilk<br>30 ml (2 tablespoons) melted butter<br>2 eggs, lightly beaten | Mix together and pour into the dry ingredients. Stir just enough to combine. |
| 2 chillies, seeded and finely chopped<br>100 g (4 oz) sweetcorn kernels, blanched<br>15 ml (1 tablespoon) chopped sun-dried tomatoes in oil | Add, mix, and pour into greased moulds or Swiss roll tin.<br>Bake in the preheated oven for 10–15 minutes until the bread is firm to the touch. Serve warm. |

Serve these, or puffs opposite, with soups, stews or salads.
If cornbread moulds are not available, bake in a Swiss roll tin of 25 × 38 cm (10 × 15 in), then cut into portions.
Herbs and vegetables such as courgettes, carrots and sweet pepper dice can be added as well.

# POTATO AND LEEK STRUDEL

**SERVES 10–12**

**OVEN:** Moderately hot, 200°C/400°F/Gas 6

| | |
|---|---|
| 1 kg (2¼ lb) small new potatoes, scrubbed | Cook in their skins until tender. Peel then cut into slices approximately 5 mm (¼ in) thick. |
| 65 g (2½ oz) butter<br>1 onion, peeled and finely chopped<br>1 garlic clove, peeled and crushed<br>2 medium leeks, washed and finely sliced | Meanwhile, sweat together until soft, about 7 minutes, then mix with the potatoes in a bowl. |
| 2 eggs, beaten<br>1 bunch of chives, finely cut<br>salt and freshly ground pepper<br>paprika and freshly grated nutmeg | Add, and season to taste with salt, pepper, paprika and nutmeg. |
| 1 quantity Strudel Pastry dough (see page 185) | Roll out. |
| 100 g (4 oz) ground almonds | Sprinkle over the dough, and spread the dough with the potato mixture.<br>Roll the pastry up into a Swiss roll shape with the filling inside, and close the sides well. |
| 50 g (2 oz) butter, melted | Brush over the strudel, then bake in the preheated oven for about 40 minutes. Serve hot. |

Cheese and blanched spinach or spinach purée can be added to the filling.

# VEGETABLE STRUDEL

**SERVES 10–12**

**OVEN:** Moderately hot, 200°C/400°F/Gas 6

| | |
|---|---|
| 1 kg (2¼ lb) large spinach leaves, washed and tough stalks removed<br>salt and freshly ground pepper | For the filling, blanch for approximately 20 seconds in boiling salted water. Rinse in cold water and allow to dry on a cloth. |
| 300 g (11 oz) vegetables according to taste (carrots, leeks, celery, shallots) | Prepare as appropriate, then cut into thin strips and blanch quickly in boiling salted water (except for the shallot). Drain. |
| 25 g (1 oz) clarified butter (see page 25)<br>freshly grated nutmeg | Melt and sweat the vegetable strips for a few minutes. Season with salt, pepper and nutmeg. |
| 1 quantity Strudel Pastry dough (see page 185) | Roll out, and arrange half the spinach thickly on it. |
| 175 g (6 oz) Fontina cheese, cut into six slices<br>6 hard-boiled eggs<br>50 g (2 oz) pine kernels<br>50 g (2 oz) alfalfa sprouts | Put half of the cheese slices on to the spinach, followed by half of the vegetable strips. Then put the whole peeled eggs, the pine kernels and sprouts on top. Top with the remaining vegetables, cheese slices and spinach.<br>Roll the pastry up into a Swiss roll shape with the filling inside. |
| 50 g (2 oz) butter, melted | Brush over the strudel. Bake for about 40 minutes in the preheated oven. Serve hot. |

The strudel may be served as a first or main course.
Many other seeds and grains apart from alfalfa can be sprouted (see page 138).

# FISH AND SEAFOOD

Fish cookery is one of my passions, and has been ever since I was a child and fished in the nearby Lake Bienne, in the foothills of the Jura in Switzerland. Wherever I travel in the world, I am drawn to the fish market and its fascinating, colourful and gleaming displays of local seafood. Even a good fishmonger, like Steve Hatt's in the Essex Road, London, is a feast for the eyes.

For those who don't eat meat, fish is the most important source of protein; even to non-vegetarians, fish is an important nutrient, as it contains so little saturated fat, is easily digested, and is rich in Vitamins A and D and fatty acids thought to be useful in protecting us from heart disease.

I have often written about fish, but every new country that I visit, I seem to learn something new about these wonderful creatures and how they can be prepared and eaten. My stay in Japan in the early 1970s was perhaps the most influential. The Japanese diet is largely composed of the very freshest fish and marine foods. Fish dishes – usually raw or very lightly cooked – are arranged beautifully on the plate with a piquant accompanying sauce, and I have adapted many of the ideas I encountered then. Japanese-style fish dishes are now very easy to prepare with all the produce available, and quite delicious to eat.

On my recent trips to Europe, I was introduced to many traditional ways with fish, not dissimilar to those I grew up with in Switzerland. There freshwater fish commonly form the basis of fish cuisine – and perch, pike, bream and carp are all favourites, along with the king of European freshwater fish, the Lake Balaton *fogash* (and the similar perch-pike, or zander).

It was on an earlier trip, to Sweden, that I learned about the glories of herring, the fish that plays such a vital role in so many of the countries bordering the North Sea, the Baltic and the Atlantic. In Britain, fresh herrings are enjoyed still, but they're usually salted or smoked; on the Continent, herrings are marin-

*Salmon tartare*

ated, salted or brined, and form a major part of many German and Scandinavian meals; it is the traditional first course of a Swedish *smörgåsbord* (buttered bread cold table).

Many fish in Britain tend to be under-rated and should be allowed to re-establish their rightful position among the more fashionable and exotic imports. Cod, for instance, can be cooked in many ways, as can the whiting. (The recipe for whiting here was a bestseller in the hotel in Montreal where I worked.) Fresh sardines or mackerel can be stuffed and baked or grilled, and crabmeat can be used to stuff vegetables and pastry. Many fish are available smoked (be careful, some are *dyed*), and these too, with their subtle flavours, can be used in a variety of ways.

# SALMON TARTARE

**SERVES 4**

| | |
|---|---|
| **300 g (11 oz) skinned and boned salmon fillet** | Chop very finely with a sharp knife, then transfer to a bowl. |
| **juice of ½ lemon**<br>**10 ml (2 teaspoons) olive oil**<br>**15 ml (1 tablespoon) finely cut chives**<br>**salt and freshly ground pepper** | Add, and mix well, seasoning to taste with salt and pepper.<br>Divide the fish mixture into four balls, and flatten them slightly. Arrange on four plates, and make a dent in the middle with your thumb. |
| **20 ml (4 teaspoons) caviar** | Place a spoonful on top of each *tartare*. |
| **a few leaves of lamb's tongue lettuce**<br>**a little lemon juice and olive oil** | Garnish with the leaves dressed with a little lemon juice and olive oil. |

As with any raw fish dish, the fish must be extremely fresh.
Serve with hot toasted slices of *baguette*.
You could also serve this accompanied by a Yoghurt Sauce with Lemon Balm (see page 75).
Lumpfish or salmon roe could replace the caviar, or the yolk of a quail's egg.

# SALMON SASHIMI

### SERVES 4

| | |
|---|---|
| about 75 ml (5 table-spoons) Sashimi Dressing (see below)<br>salt and freshly ground pepper | Lightly brush about 10 ml (2 teaspoons) over the centre of the serving plate, and season lightly with salt and pepper. |
| 350 g (12oz) salmon fillet, cut into strips approx. 5 mm (¼ in) thick | Arrange in a circle on the plate and generously brush with more dressing. |
| 20 ml (5 teaspoons) finely sliced spring onion<br>toasted sesame seeds<br>12 coriander leaves | Sprinkle over the fish to garnish, the coriander last. |

The salmon – or other fish – must be *extremely* fresh.

# SASHIMI DRESSING

| | |
|---|---|
| 25 ml (1 fl oz) *saké*<br>45 ml (3 tablespoons) *mirin* | Heat gently together, then light with a match to burn off the alcohol. |
| 1 × 2.5 cm (1 in) piece of kelp (*kombu*), wiped<br>15 ml (3 tablespoons) *tamari* sauce<br>225 ml (7½ fl oz) dark soy sauce<br>5 g (⅛ oz) loose bonito flakes | Add to the *saké* mixture, bring to the boil and simmer gently for 5 minutes. Remove from the heat and leave to stand in a cool place for at least 5–6 hours. |

All the ingredients for the dressing will be found in a Japanese or oriental supermarket.

# ROLLED OMELETTE

**SERVES 4**

| | |
|---|---|
| **8 eggs, beaten**<br>**a little vegetable stock**<br>   **(see page 24)**<br>**15 ml (1 tablespoon)**<br>   **light soy sauce**<br>**salt** | Place in a bowl and mix, seasoning to taste with salt. |
| **60 ml (4 tablespoons)**<br>   **finely grated *daikon***<br>   **radish** | Moisten and flavour with a few extra drops of soy sauce. Set aside.<br>Heat a rectangular Japanese egg pan over medium heat until hot. |
| **vegetable oil** | Lightly wipe pan with a cloth swab moistened with oil. Pour about one-third of the egg mixture into the pan, and tilt so it spreads evenly.<br>When it begins to bubble around the edges, tilt the pan up towards you and, with a pair of chopsticks, roll the egg layer towards you.<br>With the oil swab, oil the pan surface again, and push the egg roll back away from you. Add the second third of the egg mixture and tilt the pan as before, lifting the edge of the rolled omelette so that the raw mixture runs underneath.<br>When that in turn starts to set, roll as before. Oil again, pour in the last third of the mixture, cook and roll in the same way.<br>Remove from the pan and wrap in bamboo mat (if available). Press gently and let rest for a minute to shape. Unwrap and slice crosswise into 5 cm (2 in) rounds. Place two slices on each serving plate, and garnish with a mound of soy-flavoured *daikon*. |

For variation, garden peas, puréed spinach, *nori* seaweed, prawns or eel can be added to the omelette mix.

# MONKFISH PICCATA WITH COURGETTE NOODLES

**SERVES 4**

| | |
|---|---|
| 175 g (6 oz) each of green and yellow courgettes, topped and tailed | Cut with a mandoline into long strips resembling thin noodles, discarding the central core of seeds. |
| 20 × 25 g (1 oz) collops of monkfish<br>salt and freshly ground pepper<br>plain flour | Season the fish with salt and pepper, then dip into the flour. Shake off surplus. |
| 1 large egg<br>1 sachet of saffron | Beat together, then dip the collops in this. |
| 30 ml (2 tablespoons) olive oil | Heat in a non-stick pan, then fry the collops for 2–3 minutes on each side until cooked and golden brown in colour. Keep warm. |
| 275 g (10 oz) tomato *concassée* (see page 39)<br>a large sprig of thyme | Heat gently together, then add the courgette 'noodles' and season to taste with salt and pepper. Heat for about 2–3 minutes, then discard the thyme. Arrange the courgette 'noodles' and tomato on individual plates, then place the collops of fish on top. Serve immediately. |

Collop – from the French *escaloper* – is a small slice of fish (or meat). *Piccata* is the Milanese word for escalope, from the word *picchiata*, beaten (which many escalopes are before being cooked).

# Fried Fillets of Perch

**SERVES 4**

| | |
|---|---|
| **100 g (4 oz) plain flour**<br>**15 ml (1 tablespoon)**<br>**cornflour** | Sieve together into a large bowl. |
| **1 egg, separated**<br>**approx. 150 ml (5 fl oz)**<br>**water**<br>**salt and freshly ground**<br>**pepper** | Mix egg yolk and water together then incorporate into the flour. Beat to a smooth batter.<br>Whisk the egg white until stiff, then fold into the batter. Season with a pinch of salt. |
| **15 ml (1 tablespoon)**<br>**fresh chopped**<br>**parsley** | Mix into the batter. |
| **600 g (1 lb, 5 oz) fillets**<br>**of perch** | Season with salt and pepper and dust with extra flour.<br>Lightly dip the fillets into the batter. |
| **vegetable oil for deep-**<br>**frying** | Heat to 150°C/300°F, and blanch the coated fish fillets for 2 minutes. Drain and keep warm until all the pieces of fish are cooked.<br>Heat the oil to 190°C/375°F, and fry the fish again until golden and crispy brown. Drain thoroughly on kitchen paper. |
| **lemon wedges** | Serve immediately, garnished with lemon wedges. |

Fillets of perch or other fish such as sea bream, cod, salmon etc, can be cooked *en papillote*. Wrap in greaseproof paper, roasting bags or aluminium foil, and bake in a moderately hot oven, 200°C/400°F/Gas 6 for about 5–7 minutes. Add flavourings such as ginger, vegetable *julienne*, mushrooms, seasoning and a little fish stock before baking.

# PAPRIKA PIKE-PERCH WITH SAUERKRAUT

**SERVES 4**

| | |
|---|---|
| **3 sweet peppers, 1 green, 1 yellow, 1 red** | Scorch over an open flame, then peel off the skins. Remove the cores, seeds, and any white pithy ribs. Cut into strips of approximately 6 cm (2½ in) long and 5 mm (¼ in) wide. You need twelve strips of each colour. |
| **4 × 150 g (5 oz) fillets of pike-perch, trimmed**<br>**salt and freshly ground pepper** | Pat dry.<br>Take a strip of pepper and clip it on a larding needle. Insert the needle in and out of the fish (making little stitches). Alternate the colour each time, using three red, yellow and green pepper strips per fillet.<br>Season the fillets with salt and pepper, then steam for approximately 4–5 minutes. |
| **1 quantity *Sauerkraut* (see page 94)** | Warm through gently, and serve the fish immediately on a bed of cabbage. |

The pike-perch, or zander, is a predatory freshwater fish beloved of anglers in the Balkans. Fish in Hungary have been known to grow to 13.5 kg (30 lb) in weight; smaller ones are common in Rumania.
The fish is also central to many of the Balkan cuisines. Use a pike or a perch, or any firm-fleshed freshwater fish.

# TATAKI

**SERVES 4**

| | |
|---|---|
| **500 g (18 oz) very fresh tuna or salmon fillet, in the piece**<br>**salt and freshly ground pepper**<br>**vegetable oil** | Season the fish with salt and pepper. Scorch or sear the surfaces of the fillet over a very hot gas flame, or in a heavy non-stick pan greased with a few drops of oil. Cool immediately in iced water, drain and pat dry. |
| **20 ml (4 teaspoons) English mustard** | Lightly brush all over the fish. |
| **15 ml (1 tablespoon) finely chopped fresh ginger**<br>**10 basil leaves, finely cut**<br>**4 spring onions, finely chopped** | Mix together, then press all over the fish fillet. Cut the fish into 5 mm (¼ in) slices, and arrange neatly on individual serving plates. |
| **1 head chicory, cut into 3 cm (1¼ in) strips**<br>**1 ripe avocado pear, peeled, stoned and thinly sliced**<br>**juice of ½ lemon** | Season with salt, pepper and lemon juice, and arrange in little mounds on the plates. |
| **1 ripe beef tomato, skinned, seeded and cut into 5 mm (¼ in) dice**<br>**4 sprigs of chervil, picked** | Garnish with tomato dice and chervil leaves. Serve immediately. |

Serve with the Lemon Soy Sauce on page 75.
You could also just sear the (very fresh) fish as above, and serve it with pickled vegetables and a dipping sauce (Lemon Soy again).

*Tuna tataki with pickled vegetables*

# Marinated Herrings

**SERVES 4**

1 kg (2¼ lb) herrings,
  scaled, cleaned, and
  heads, tails and fins
  removed
30 ml (2 tablespoons)
  salt

Lay the herrings in a dish, sprinkle with the salt, and
leave for about 2 hours.
Rinse in cold water, and peel away the silvery skins.
Cut each herring into three or four pieces.

---

30 ml (2 tablespoons)
  vegetable oil

Heat in a heavy pan and sauté the fish for 3–4
minutes on each side until golden.
Remove the fish from the pan and allow to drain.
Place in a deep dish.

---

300 ml (10 fl oz) water
200 ml (7 fl oz) white
  wine vinegar
1 medium carrot,
  peeled, scored and
  thinly sliced
2 shallots, peeled and
  cut into fine rings
5 ml (1 teaspoon)
  mustard seeds
a few black
  peppercorns, crushed
1 bay leaf
2 sprigs of thyme
1 sprig of rosemary

Bring to the boil together in a large saucepan, then
allow to cool.
Pour over the fish, cover and leave to marinate for at
least 2 hours before serving.

---

a few sprigs of dill

Serve the fish garnished with dill.

---

This recipe is inspired by the herring dishes I encountered when
working in Sweden. The Scandinavians marinate many of their
perfectly fresh fish – think of *gravadlax*, marinated salmon.

# YOUNG SALTED HERRING SALAD

**SERVES 4**

| | |
|---|---|
| **400 g (14 oz) *matjes* or sweet pickled herrings** | Cut into small pieces, and place in a bowl. |
| **1 small onion, peeled and finely chopped** **150 ml (5 fl oz) soured cream** **30 ml (2 tablespoons) finely cut chives** **salt and freshly ground pepper** | Add, keeping 5 ml (1 teaspoon) of the chives to use as garnish. Season with salt and pepper if necessary. Bind well together, then transfer to a clean dish. |
| **1 red apple, cored, quartered and thinly sliced** **1 shallot, peeled and cut into rings** **paprika** | Garnish with the thinly sliced apples, shallot rings, paprika and reserved chives. |

 Slices of *pumpernickel* or brown bread are particularly good with this dish.
Beetroot too will go well.
You can use *fromage frais* instead of soured cream.

# Char-Grilled Swordfish Steak 'Niçoise'

**SERVES 4**

4 × 150 g (5 oz)
swordfish steaks
1 garlic clove, peeled
and finely crushed
with 2.5 ml (½
teaspoon) salt
a few black
peppercorns, crushed
75 ml (5 tablespoons)
olive oil

Rub the swordfish steaks with the garlic, salt, black pepper and 15 ml (1 tablespoon) of the oil.
Char-grill for 3–5 minutes on each side, depending on the thickness of the steaks.

1 anchovy fillet, finely
chopped
30 ml (2 tablespoons)
red wine vinegar
10 black brine-cured
olives, pitted and
quartered
10 ml (2 teaspoons)
capers, roughly
chopped
30 ml (2 tablespoons)
mixed sweet peppers,
seeded and cut into
5 mm (¼ in) dice
15 ml (1 tablespoon)
finely cut fresh flat
parsley
30 ml (2 tablespoons)
finely chopped
spring onions

For the Niçoise oil, mix together the remaining ingredients. Season to taste with salt and pepper. Transfer the swordfish steaks to individual plates, and lace with the oil.

You could also use tuna or monkfish in this recipe.
You could make brochettes with the fish – delicious for a barbecue, or to take on a picnic.

*Swordfish steak 'Niçoise'*

# COULIBIAC

**SERVES 8–10**

**OVEN: Moderately hot, 190°C/375°F/Gas 5**

Grease the *reverse*, unlipped, side of a baking tray
approximately 23–25 × 33–35 cm (9–10 × 13–14 in).

| | |
|---|---|
| 15 ml (1 tablespoon) olive oil<br>1 small onion, peeled and finely chopped | Heat together in a casserole, and cook gently for 2 minutes without colouring the onion. |
| 165 g (5½ oz) long-grain rice<br>300 ml (10 fl oz) fish stock (see page 24)<br>1 sprig of thyme<br>1 bay leaf<br>salt and freshly ground pepper | Stir in, and season with a little salt and pepper. Bring to the boil, then cover with a greased piece of paper. Cook in the preheated oven for about 15 minutes. When ready, transfer the drained rice to a tray, spreading it out so that it can cool. Remove herbs. |
| 15 ml (1 tablespoon) olive oil<br>150 g (5 oz) button mushrooms, wiped and sliced | Meanwhile, heat together in a frying pan, then fry until almost dry. |
| 50 ml (2 fl oz) dry white wine<br>250 ml (8 fl oz) double cream | Add, and continue to simmer until reduced to a thick consistency.<br>Place the rice in a bowl, and bind with the cream mixture. |
| 30 ml (2 tablespoons) finely cut chives | Stir in, and adjust the seasoning. |
| 1 quantity Brioche dough (see page 184) | Roll out one-third to the size of the baking tray, approximately 3 mm (⅛ in) thick. Place on the greased reverse of the baking tray. |
| 1 egg, beaten | Brush some over the rolled-out brioche dough. |

| | |
|---|---|
| 4 × 20–23 cm (8–9 in) round herb pancakes (see page 193) | Arrange two of the pancakes, slightly overlapping, in the centre of the rolled brioche. Spread on one-third of the rice mixture, making a neat layer, and leaving a 3 cm (1¼ in) border all round (roughly the same size as the fish fillets). |
| 6 medium-hard boiled eggs (about 7 minutes), sliced with an egg slicer 2 × 750 g (1 lb, 10 oz) pieces smoked haddock (or salmon) fillet, skinned and boned | Build up more layers using half of the sliced egg, a piece of fish, and another third of the rice, followed by the second piece of fish, remaining egg and rice. Cover with the remaining pancakes and tuck them neatly under the filling, shaping to make a tidy and firm topping. Roll out the remaining larger piece of brioche dough to roughly 1½ times the size of the original piece. Brush the edges of the brioche with beaten egg, and lift the top piece with the aid of a rolling pin. Ease it into position, and lightly press all round to seal. Trim the excess pastry at the edges. You can flute the edges with your thumb and forefinger, with a pastry tweezer, or simply press with the tines of a fork. Brush all over with egg wash and decorate the top with leftover brioche dough. Bake in the preheated oven for 35–40 minutes until golden brown. Serve immediately. |

The smoked haddock (or salmon) could first be marinated with about 30 ml (2 tablespoons) olive oil, squeeze of lemon juice, and some finely cut dill for 30–60 minutes.
You could use puff pastry instead of the brioche dough.
You can prepare the brioche dough and pancakes the day before. The coulibiac itself could be prepared in advance and baked at the last minute.
Baking on the *reverse* side of the baking tray makes the coulibiac (and similar items) easier to handle when cooked. You simply slide it off the tray – because there is no lip – without having to lift, which might break or damage the pastry.

# BAKED WHITING WITH POTATO AND ONIONS

**SERVES 4**

**OVEN:** Moderately hot, 190°C/375°F/Gas 5

| | |
|---|---|
| **4 medium potatoes, peeled** | Finely slice, and lay at one side of a shallow, heatproof baking dish. Flatten them using the palm of your hand, arc-ing them out, along one side of the dish. |
| **2 medium red onions, peeled** | Cut in half and finely slice, then flatten as for the potatoes. Do this at the other side of the dish. |
| **1 whiting, approx. 1 kg (2¼ lb) in weight, cleaned, gutted and gills removed**<br>**salt and freshly ground pepper** | Season with salt and pepper inside and out, and place in the centre of the dish. Season the potatoes and onion as well. |
| **200 g (7 oz) fennel bulb, finely sliced** | Stuff into the whiting. |
| **250 ml (8 fl oz) fish stock (see page 24)**<br>**50 ml (2 fl oz) dry white wine** | Pour half over to barely cover the fish. Bring the dish to the boil on top of the stove for 2–3 minutes, then bake in the preheated oven for another 25–30 minutes, adding more liquid gradually, until the potatoes and fish are cooked. |
| **15 ml (1 tablespoon) olive oil** | Brush over the fish to give it a shiny glaze, and serve immediately. |

*Overleaf: Baked whiting with potato and onions*

# CRABMEAT SAMOSAS

**MAKES ABOUT 24**

**OVEN:** Moderate, 180°C/350°F/Gas 4

| | |
|---|---|
| 1 shallot, peeled and finely chopped 30 ml (2 tablespoons) sesame oil | Sweat together until the shallot is soft. |
| 1 small fennel bulb or cucumber, diced | Add, and cook for 2 minutes. |
| 1 red chilli, seeded and finely sliced 200 g (7 oz) crab meat, flaked salt and pepper | Add, and season to taste with salt and pepper. |
| 5 ml (1 teaspoon) each of finely cut chives and tarragon | Add, remove from the heat and cool. |
| 6 filo pastry sheets | Lay on top of each other. Cut them all simultaneously into 4 cm (1½ in) wide strips. |
| 50 g (2 oz) butter, melted | Brush over the strips. Place a spoonful of the crab mixture on the top corner of one of the pastry strips. Fold over into a triangle and fold over again and again until you have reached the end of the pastry strip, ending up with a tight triangle package. Place on a baking sheet. Continue, using remaining filo, butter and filling. |
| egg yolk sesame, poppy or fennel seeds | When all are ready, brush the tops with egg wash and sprinkle with sesame, poppy or fennel seeds. Bake in the preheated oven for 10–12 minutes until puffed up and golden in colour. |

Serve as a snack, two or three as a starter with one of the sauces in this chapter, perhaps, or as a finger food with drinks. There are a variety of fillings you can use: Stilton and Spinach; goat or Feta cheese with leek and parsley; stir-fried vegetables; seafood and rice.

# GRILLED SARDINES STUFFED WITH ONION AND CAPERS

**SERVES 4**

| | |
|---|---|
| 1 onion, peeled and finely chopped<br>15 ml (1 tablespoon) olive oil | Gently sweat together until the onion has softened a little. Remove from the heat. |
| 90 ml (6 tablespoons) chopped parsley<br>45 ml (3 tablespoons) capers, drained and chopped<br>1 strip of lemon peel, finely chopped<br>salt and freshly ground pepper<br>a small pinch of cayenne pepper | Mix together with the onion, and season to taste with salt, pepper and cayenne. |
| 12 sardines, scaled and gutted<br>lemon juice to taste | With a teaspoon, gently stuff this mixture into the sardines, then arrange them in a heatproof dish. If there is any stuffing leftover, make this into a bed, or sprinkle on top. Season the fish with salt, pepper and lemon juice.<br>Place under a hot grill for about 4–5 minutes, depending on size. Turn over halfway through the cooking time.<br>Spoon the juices over the sardines and serve. |

Onions and capers go very well with the hearty flavour of sardines. If you like you can cook small mackerel in this way. The sardines (or mackerel) are good for the barbecue.

*Grilled sardines stuffed with onion and capers*

# BEEF TOMATO WITH CRAB MEAT, FROMAGE FRAIS SAUCE

**SERVES 4**

| | |
|---|---|
| **4 beef tomatoes**<br>**salt and pepper** | Cut the top off the tomatoes, scoop out the pulp, and lightly salt. Invert to drain until ready to fill. |
| **1 small shallot, peeled and finely chopped**<br>**2.5 ml (½ teaspoon) Dijon mustard**<br>**45 ml (3 tablespoons) lemon juice**<br>**100 ml (3½ fl oz) olive oil** | For the dressing, mix together, seasoning with some salt and pepper. |
| **1 avocado, peeled** | Cut flesh into thin slices. Season with salt, pepper and some of the dressing. |
| **250 g (9 oz) white crab meat, flaked**<br>**15 ml (1 tablespoon) freshly cut mixed herbs (basil, tarragon)** | Mix together, season with salt and pepper, and moisten with some of the dressing.<br>Brush the insides of the tomato shells with the dressing. Fill with alternate layers of avocado and crab meat. |
| **100 ml (3½ fl oz) fromage frais**<br>**milk**<br>**15 ml (1 tablespoon) finely cut chives**<br>**cayenne pepper** | For the sauce, thin down the *fromage frais* with milk to a sauce consistency, then add the chives, some salt and pepper and cayenne. |
| **4 sprigs of basil** | Serve each tomato on a bed of the sauce, and garnish with a sprig of basil. |

*Fromage frais*, also known as *fromage blanc*, is a very low fat fresh curd cheese. *Fromage blanc* in France is the family name for all fresh cheeses, even when full-fat.

*Beef tomato with crab meat and fromage frais sauce*

# STUFFED COURGETTES

**SERVES 4**

| | |
|---|---|
| 8 medium courgettes, peeled | Hollow out the centres as you would an apple. Keep aside until required. |
| 100 g (4 oz) king prawns<br>100 g (4 oz) crab meat<br>4 waterchestnuts<br>1 small egg<br>15 ml (1 tablespoon) sesame oil<br>salt and pepper | Shell and devein the prawns, flake the crab meat, and roughly chop the chestnuts.<br>Place everything in the food processor, and process for a few seconds to a smooth paste. Remove from the processor, and season with salt and pepper. |
| 30 ml (2 tablespoons) finely chopped spring onions | Mix in, and spoon the mixture into a piping bag with a plain tube, about 1 cm (½ in) in diameter. Pipe into the hollowed-out courgettes. |
| 2 shallots, peeled<br>1 garlic clove, peeled<br>15 ml (1 tablespoon) olive oil<br>5 ml (1 teaspoon) finely chopped fresh ginger | Chop the shallots finely and crush the garlic.<br>Sweat all together in a large shallow pan until soft. |
| 500 ml (18 fl oz) vegetable stock (see page 24) | Add, and bring to the boil. Place the stuffed courgettes in the liquid and simmer very gently for approximately 15 minutes. |
| 100 g (4 oz) leeks, cut into rings<br>1 medium carrot, finely sliced | Add to the liquid and cook for a further 5 minutes until the stuffing is cooked. Lift the courgettes out and keep warm. |
| 5 ml (1 teaspoon) cornflour<br>soy sauce<br>chopped coriander | Reduce and thicken the liquid with a little cornflour. Add soy sauce to taste, and check seasoning. Lightly coat the courgettes with the sauce, garnish with leek and carrot, and sprinkle with coriander. |

Almost any vegetable can be used in this way. Try small kohlrabi or turnips, cucumbers or courgette flowers.

# Smoked Trout Scones

**MAKES 12–15 SCONES**

**OVEN:** Moderately hot, 190°C/375°F/Gas 5

| | |
|---|---|
| **250 g (9 oz) smoked trout fillets, flaked**<br>**½ bunch spring onions, finely chopped**<br>**finely grated zest of 1 lemon** | Combine in a bowl. |
| **250 g (9 oz) plain flour**<br>**30 ml (2 tablespoons) baking powder** | Sift together into a mixing bowl. |
| **30 g (1¼ oz) unsalted butter** | Rub into the flour until the mixture resembles fine breadcrumbs. Fold in the trout mixture. |
| **2 eggs, lightly beaten**<br>**150 ml (5 fl oz) milk or single cream (or a mixture)** | Combine, and pour into the flour mixture. Gently bring to a dough with a palette knife.<br>Turn the mixture out on to a lightly floured board, and pat the dough out with the palm of your hand until approximately 2 cm (¾ in) thick. Cut into rounds with a plain round cutter about 4–5 cm (1½–2 in) in diameter. |
| **1 egg yolk** | Place the scones on a baking sheet and brush the tops with egg wash. Bake in the preheated oven for 10–15 minutes until golden. |

Serve warm on their own, or garnished with soured cream and finely cut chives. Good with a fish salad or soup instead of bread.

The scones could be made of half and half plain and wholemeal flour.

# Yoghurt Sauce with Lemon Balm

| | |
|---|---|
| 15 g (½ oz) lemon balm | Pluck the leaves from the stalks, and chop the leaves finely. |

| | |
|---|---|
| 300 g (11 oz) natural yoghurt<br>grated rind and juice of ½ lemon<br>50 ml (2 fl oz) double cream<br>15 ml (1 tablespoon) lemon (or fruit) vinegar<br>salt and freshly ground pepper | Mix together and season with salt and pepper. Work in the finely chopped lemon balm. |

Serve with fish tartare (see page 50) or barbecued fish, or as a salad sauce.

# Lemon Soy Sauce

| | |
|---|---|
| 105 ml (7 tablespoons) lemon juice<br>105 ml (7 tablespoons) soy sauce<br>75 ml (5 tablespoons) rice vinegar<br>5 g (⅛ oz) bonito flakes<br>2 cm (¾ in) length of kelp (*kombu*) | Combine all the ingredients together. Mix well and leave in the refrigerator overnight.<br>Strain and use as required. |

Serve with Tuna Tataki (see page 56) as a dipping sauce.

# COOKED VEGETABLE DISHES

For those who don't eat meat, vegetables must form the basis of the diet, with other foods like fish, milk and milk products like cheese providing additional flavours, textures and proteins. To many, vegetarian food is dull, with its soya-based meat substitutes and nut-based meat look-alikes. However, with the wealth of fresh and delicious produce now available to us all year round, there is no excuse for eating boring food. Vegetables are colourful, full of flavour if cooked correctly, and have interesting textures; they can be combined with other vegetables, pulses and grains, protein foods and a variety of herb and spice flavourings. I hope that the following selection of recipes – for main-course and starter dishes, for snacks, and for accompanying vegetable dishes – will inspire you to new heights of invention.

Once again, I have been inspired by Europe, and the wealth of traditional recipes there. Just as vegetable soups are staples all over Europe, so too are vegetable amalgams in vegetable stews and dishes like *peperonata*, the Italian version of *ratatouille*. Italy has also been the inspiration in the use of *pesto* – made with parsley or, more traditionally, basil – with a sturdy and meaty vegetable such as aubergine (the sauce is also very good with home-made pasta and on pizzas). Pumpkin stews and soups and potato dishes of all kinds are very typical of Central Europe: variations on potato cakes are found in Switzerland (*rösti*), Holland, Poland, Germany and all over the British Isles. Potatoes are also used in dumplings in Central Europe and in *gnocchi* in Italy.

I encountered *sauerkraut* in the Balkan countries, but it was familiar to me anyway, coming from the German part of Switzerland. However, the practice of salting down cabbage and leaving it to ferment is not particularly German: the Romans did it, and

*Potato cakes and Cherry tomato compote*

every other cabbage-growing country too – think of the *choucroûtes* of Alsace-Lorraine.

Hungary was the inspiration for my mushroom *goulash* or *gulyas*, using paprika, the spice obtained from dried powdered red capsicum peppers. I was introduced to many of the secrets of paprika, and other Hungarian specialities, by Zoltan Halasz, the famous food expert and cookbook writer. He told me that there is a much greater variety of pepper, thus of spice, available in Hungary than there is in Britain; the spices there range from 'exquisite delicate' (mild enough for invalids) to hot (the equivalent of cayenne pepper, so *very* hot).

The chilli peppers from which cayenne is derived lend their bite to some vegetable stews which are rather more eastern in origin. And Hungary again inspired my red pepper sauce, as useful as tomato for accompanying pasta and fish and topping pizzas.

# POTATO CAKES

### SERVES 4

| | |
|---|---|
| **500 g (18 oz) potatoes, peeled**<br>**salt** | Cook in a pan of boiling salted water until soft, then drain well and mash into a bowl. |
| **25 g (1 oz) unsalted butter**<br>**2 egg yolks** | Stir in and mix well. |
| **2 spring onions, finely chopped**<br>**15 ml (1 tablespoon) roughly chopped coriander**<br>**65 g (2½ oz) Cheddar cheese, grated**<br>**freshly ground pepper**<br>**freshly grated nutmeg** | Add, and season to taste with salt, pepper and nutmeg.<br>Roll the mixture into a log, then divide into eight pieces. |
| **plain flour**<br>**1 egg, beaten**<br>**65 g (2½ oz) fresh breadcrumbs or chopped nuts** | Roll and shape into cakes on a lightly floured board. Dip in the beaten egg and then in the breadcrumbs or nuts (you may require *more* of the latter).<br>Chill in the refrigerator to firm. |
| **60 ml (4 tablespoons) olive oil** | Heat in a pan and pan-fry the cakes for approximately 3–5 minutes on both sides until heated through and golden brown in colour. |

Serve with Cherry Tomato Compote (see page 95). The cakes are also good served as the base for, or at the side of, Spiced Aubergine and Okra Stew (see page 87).

# ANNA POTATOES WITH WILD MUSHROOMS

**SERVES 8**

**OVEN:** Moderate, 180°C/350°F/Gas 4

| | |
|---|---|
| about 85ml (3 floz) olive oil<br>1 shallot, peeled and finely chopped<br>1 garlic clove, peeled and finely chopped | Heat 30 ml (2 tablespoons) of the oil in a large saucepan, and sweat the shallot and garlic for a few minutes. |
| 500g (18 oz) assorted wild mushrooms, washed and sliced<br>15 ml (1 tablespoon) finely cut chives<br>15 ml (1 tablespoon) finely cut basil<br>salt and freshly ground pepper | Add, and season with salt and pepper. Cook for 2 minutes to soften. Transfer to a colander to drain off any excess cooking juices.<br>Heat a 20-23 cm (8-9 in) anna potato mould (see below), and brush with a little of the remaining oil. |
| 1 kg (2¼ lb) potatoes, peeled, sliced into paper-thin slices, washed and dried | Line the bottom of the mould with a layer of potato slices, arranging them in concentric circles, overlapping slightly. Season with a little salt and pepper. |
| 90 ml (6 tablespoons) grated Sbrinz or Parmesan cheese | Sprinkle a little over the potato slices, along with a spoonful of the mushroom mixture, and drizzle with a little of the olive oil.<br>Repeat this procedure until you reach the top of the mould, finishing with a layer of the potatoes.<br>Bake in the preheated oven for approximately 1-1½ hours.<br>Press down with a metal spatula every 15 minutes.<br>Leave the potatoes to cool down for 5-6 minutes, then run a small sharp knife around the edges of the mould to loosen. Turn out and serve. Flash under a hot grill if not brown. |

 Anna potatoes are usually cooked in a special heat and ovenproof metal dish. If you don't have one, use a charlotte mould or a straight-sided deep dish.

# BROCCOLI MOUSSE WITH WALNUT GOAT CHEESE SAUCE

**SERVES 4**

**OVEN:** Moderate, 180°C/350°F/Gas 4

| | |
|---|---|
| 300 g (11 oz) broccoli, cut into pieces<br>15 ml (1 tablespoon) olive oil | Sweat together in a saucepan for a few minutes. |
| 200 ml (7 fl oz) vegetable stock (see page 24)<br>salt and freshly ground pepper<br>freshly grated nutmeg | Add and season with salt, pepper and nutmeg. Cook until soft, about 10 minutes.<br>Blend in a food processor until a fine purée. |
| 2 large eggs, beaten<br>50 ml (2 fl oz) double cream | Add, and correct seasoning.<br>Pour the mixture into four greased 150 ml (5 fl oz) moulds, and cook in a *bain-marie* in the preheated oven for approximately 35–40 minutes. |
| ½ quantity Walnut Goat Cheese Sauce (see page 164)<br>8 tiny florets of broccoli, lightly sautéed in butter | Turn out of the moulds, and serve with the sauce.<br>Garnish with the broccoli florets. |

Serve the mousses hot or cold as a starter.
For the photograph, we wrapped the mousse in cling film, placed in a mould, and steamed it for a little longer than above.

*Broccoli mousse with walnut goat cheese sauce*

# EGG AND SPINACH IN JACKET POTATOES

**SERVES 4**

**OVEN:** Moderately hot, 200°C/400°F/Gas 6

| | |
|---|---|
| 4 large potatoes, scrubbed | Place on a baking tray and bake in the preheated oven for 1–1¼ hours until soft. Remove from the oven and cut a slice from the top of each potato carefully; scoop out the soft potato flesh with a spoon, taking care not to tear the skin. |
| 30 g (1¼ oz) unsalted butter salt and freshly ground pepper | Mash into the flesh and season to taste. Divide the mixture between the potato skins and press down well leaving a hollow in the centre. |
| 100 g (4 oz) spinach, washed, tough stalks removed and blanched freshly grated nutmeg | Quickly heat, and season with salt, pepper and nutmeg. Divide between the four hollows. |
| 4 eggs | Break into the four spinach-lined hollows. Return to the oven for about 6–8 minutes to set. Serve immediately. |

A miniature version of this can be made using small new potatoes and quail's eggs.

# MUSHROOM KEBABS

**SERVES 4**

| | |
|---|---|
| 450 g (1 lb) large button mushrooms salt and freshly ground pepper | Place in a colander and sprinkle with 2.5 ml (½ teaspoon) salt. Mix well and leave to drain for 30 minutes. Rinse in cold water and blot dry. Thread the mushrooms on to four to eight skewers. Place in a tray. |

| 30 ml (2 tablespoons) lemon juice<br>15 ml (1 tablespoon) light soy sauce<br>15 ml (1 tablespoon) *saké*<br>10 ml (2 teaspoons) caster sugar | Heat together, adding a little pepper, then leave to cool.<br>Pour over the mushroom kebabs, and leave to marinate for another 30–60 minutes.<br>Cook on a barbecue or under a grill, basting occasionally with the marinade. |

| 30 ml (2 tablespoons) chopped spring onions | Serve immediately, sprinkled with the chopped spring onion. |

**M** Serve as a starter, a canapé or vegetable accompaniment. They'd be good to take on a picnic.

# SWEET POTATOES WITH SOURED CREAM AND CHIVES

**SERVES 4**

| 500 g (18 oz) sweet potatoes, scrubbed and cut into rounds 2 cm (¾ in) thick<br>2 pieces of lemon peel<br>a pinch of salt<br>15 ml (1 tablespoon) caster sugar | Place in a saucepan, barely cover with water, and cook until soft, approximately 15 minutes. Drain. |

| 100 ml (3½ fl oz) soured cream<br>30 ml (2 tablespoons) finely chopped chives | Mix together, and serve with the cooked sweet potatoes. |

# Wild Mushroom Goulash

**SERVES 4**

45 ml (3 tablespoons)
  olive oil
1 large garlic clove,
  peeled and finely
  chopped
2 shallots, peeled and
  finely chopped

Sweat together in a frying pan for 2 minutes.

---

500 g (18 oz) assorted
  wild mushrooms

Stir in, adding the firmer varieties first. Sauté over a high heat until the mushrooms start to go soft.

---

200 g (7 oz) tomato
  concasseé (see page 39)
30 ml (2 tablespoons)
  celeriac leaves,
  roughly chopped
salt and freshly ground
  pepper
paprika

Add, and season to taste with salt, pepper and paprika. Warm through and serve immediately.

---

Add paprika to taste – in Hungary there are about six varieties to choose from, varying in heat.
In Hungary, we used the leaves from celeriac roots; use celery leaves or flat parsley or whatever you have available.

*Wild mushroom goulash*

# CHICORY AND MUSHROOMS WITH CHEESE

**SERVES 4**

| | |
|---|---|
| **4 large heads of chicory**<br>**150 g (5 oz) small button mushrooms** | Wash the chicory well, cut a slice off the root end and separate the leaves. Wash the mushrooms well. Place the chicory in one non-stick saucepan, the mushrooms in another. |
| **120 ml (4 fl oz) vegetable stock (see page 24)**<br>**10 ml (2 teaspoons) lemon juice** | Divide between the two pans. |
| **5 ml (1 teaspoon) honey** | Add to the chicory.<br>Cook the chicory quickly for 1–2 minutes until just tender. Drain, reserving the stock, and arrange the chicory in a small gratin dish.<br>Reduce the stock by boiling to 15 ml (1 tablespoon), and pour over the chicory.<br>Sauté the mushrooms quickly until the liquid has disappeared. Spoon the mushrooms over the chicory in the dish. |
| **salt and freshly ground pepper** | Season to taste. |
| **65 g (2½ oz) Gouda cheese, grated** | Sprinkle over the vegetables, and bubble under a hot grill until golden. |

A delicious way of serving chicory, usually served raw as a salad vegetable.

# Spiced Aubergine and Okra Stew

**SERVES 4**

1 large onion, peeled and finely chopped
2 large garlic cloves, peeled and finely chopped
5 ml (1 teaspoon) finely chopped fresh ginger
50 ml (2 fl oz) vegetable oil

Sweat together in a large saucepan until soft.

---

5 cardamom seeds, crushed
5 ml (1 teaspoon) each of ground coriander and ground cumin
2.5 ml (½ teaspoon) each of turmeric and paprika
2 chilli peppers, seeded and roughly chopped

Add, stirring, and cook for 2 minutes.

---

2 aubergines, approx. 500 g (18 oz), cut into 2 cm (¾ in) chunks
250 g (9 oz) small okra, trimmed
1 × 400 g (14 oz) can plum tomatoes, roughly chopped
120 ml (4 fl oz) vegetable stock (see page 24)
salt and freshly ground pepper

Add, along with the tomato liquid, and mix well with the spices. Season with salt and pepper.
Bring the mixture to a simmer, then cover and cook, stirring frequently, for 35–40 minutes until the aubergine and okra are cooked and the stew is thick.

---

30 ml (2 tablespoons) roughly chopped fresh coriander

Taste to check the seasoning, and then add the coriander.

---

This would be delicious served with Bulgur, Peas and Sweetcorn (see page 108).

# BREADED AUBERGINE

**SERVES 4**

**OVEN:** Moderately hot, 200°C/400°F/Gas 6

| | |
|---|---|
| 45 ml (3 tablespoons) mixed chopped herbs (thyme, rosemary, parsley and sage)<br>1 small garlic clove, peeled and crushed<br>100 g (4 oz) wholemeal breadcrumbs | Mix together. |
| 1 egg<br>salt and freshly ground pepper | Beat, adding some salt and pepper to taste. |
| 1 large aubergine, about 250 g (9 oz) | Wash and dry, then slice into 5 mm (¼ in) slices (about 20 altogether).<br>Turn these slices first in beaten egg and then in the breadcrumb mixture. |
| 45–60 ml (3–4 tablespoons) olive oil | Heat and shallow-fry the aubergines on both sides over a medium heat until golden and crisp. Drain well on kitchen paper. Or you could bake them for 15 minutes in the preheated oven, drizzled with a little olive oil. |

These aubergine slices go very well with the Roasted Red Pepper Sauce on page 97. They could be served as an accompanying vegetable, and would be delicious simply served with a salad.

# AUBERGINE WITH PARSLEY PESTO

### SERVES 4

**2 medium aubergines, cut lengthwise into 5 mm (¼ in) slices**
**7.5 ml (1½ teaspoons) salt**

Arrange in one layer in a colander or on a rack set over a tray. Sprinkle evenly with salt on both sides. Leave to stand and sweat for 1–2 hours.

**1 garlic clove, peeled and roughly chopped**
**25 g (1 oz) parsley leaves**
**30 ml (2 tablespoons) pine kernels**
**25 g (1 oz) Parmesan cheese, finely grated**
**100 ml (3½ fl oz) olive oil**

For the pesto, place all the ingredients in a liquidiser and purée to a fine paste.

**60 ml (4 tablespoons) olive oil**

Rinse and dry the aubergine slices with kitchen paper. Brush with some of the olive oil and grill on both sides until tender and golden brown in colour (about 7–8 minutes, turning once).

**2 tomatoes, skinned, seeded and cut into 5 mm (¼ in) dice**
**freshly ground black pepper**
**30 ml (2 tablespoons) grated Parmesan cheese**

To serve, drizzle the aubergines with the parsley pesto, then sprinkle with the tomato, freshly ground black pepper, and lastly, the Parmesan. It is best served at room temperature.

The aubergines are delicious without the pesto. Garnish with a few thin onion rings, tomato *concassée* (see page 39) and freshly chopped parsley.
You may not use all the parsley pesto. Store any left over, well sealed, in the refrigerator for a couple of days.
For a conventional pesto, simply replace the parsley with fresh basil.

# PARSNIP CROQUETTES

**SERVES 4–6**

1 kg (2¼ lb) parsnips, peeled and thinly sliced
salt and freshly ground pepper

Cook in boiling salted water until tender, approximately 10 minutes. Drain thoroughly and rub through a sieve.

50 g (2 oz) unsalted butter
5 ml (1 teaspoon) curry powder
freshly grated nutmeg

Beat in, then taste for seasoning, adding salt, pepper and nutmeg. Allow to cool, then roll into croquettes about 4 cm (1½ in) long and 1 cm (½ in) wide (you should have 12 to 14).

plain flour
1–2 eggs, beaten
75–100 g (3–4 oz) fresh white breadcrumbs

Dip first in the flour and then the beaten egg, then roll in the breadcrumbs. Leave to rest in the refrigerator for approximately 1 hour.

vegetable oil for deep-frying

Deep-fry in plenty of hot oil for approximately 3–4 minutes until golden brown. Drain well on kitchen paper and serve while hot.

These can be served as a vegetable accompaniment, but would be delicious with Cherry Tomato Compote (see page 95) as a starter.

# ORIENTAL PUMPKIN AND GREEN BEAN STEW

**SERVES 4–6**

| | |
|---|---|
| 2 garlic cloves, peeled<br>2 slices fresh ginger, peeled<br>2 fresh red chilli peppers, seeded and sliced<br>15 ml (1 tablespoon) fermented black beans, rinsed | Grind together to a paste. |
| 30 ml (2 tablespoons) vegetable oil<br>2 shallots, peeled and finely chopped | Heat together in a deep frying pan and gently fry along with the chilli paste for 3–4 minutes. |
| 400 g (14 oz) pumpkin or squash flesh, cut in chunks | Add, and mix it with the paste. Cover with a lid, and stew for 5 minutes. |
| 200 ml (7 fl oz) vegetable stock (see page 24) or water | Add half the stock and cook until tender, approximately 10 minutes. |
| 250 g (9 oz) green beans, prepared (use young runners, French etc) | Add, and cook for a further 5–7 minutes, adding more stock if necessary. |
| 30 ml (2 tablespoons) soy sauce<br>30 ml (2 tablespoons) roughly chopped fresh coriander | Season to taste with soy sauce, and serve garnished with coriander. |

The Japanese Kabocha type squash is best suited for this recipe. It is unusually thick-fleshed, sweet and richly flavoured. Fermented black beans are preserved soy beans; they are very dark in colour and very salty.

# Braised Pumpkin with Lentils

**SERVES 4–6**

| | |
|---|---|
| 120 g (4½ oz) continental lentils, soaked overnight | Drain, then cover with fresh cold water, and cook until tender, about 30–35 minutes. Drain. |
| 750 g (1 lb, 10 oz) pumpkin | Meanwhile, peel and remove seeds, and cottony fibres. Cut the flesh into small neat wedges. |
| 30 ml (2 tablespoons) vegetable oil<br>4 shallots, peeled and cut into rings<br>1 large garlic clove, peeled and sliced | Sweat together for 2–3 minutes, then stir in the pumpkin. |
| salt and pepper<br>a pinch of sugar | Season with salt, pepper and sugar.<br>Mix the pumpkin mixture with the lentils. |
| 1 × 400 g (14 oz) can plum tomatoes and their juice<br>a sprig of thyme<br>1 bay leaf | Add, and cook together for another 20 minutes until the pumpkin is soft and tender. |
| vegetable stock (see page 24) | Add some stock if necessary. The mixture should be quite moist but not runny. |
| 15 ml (1 tablespoon) finely cut parsley | Correct seasoning and serve sprinkled with the parsley. |

Use green or brown lentils – also known as continental lentils – or, preferably, *lentilles du Puy*. These are said to be the finest, grown in the volcanic soil around Puy de Dôme in the Auvergne. They have a good earthy taste.
Pick over the lentils before soaking to remove any tiny stones.

From top: *Oriental pumpkin and green bean stew, and Braised pumpkin with lentils*

# SAUERKRAUT

**SERVES 4**

| | |
|---|---|
| 30 ml (2 tablespoons) olive oil<br>1 onion, peeled and finely chopped<br>1 garlic clove, peeled and crushed | Cook gently together until soft. |
| 500 g (18 oz) *sauerkraut*, rinsed if necessary | Add, and stir to mix with the oil and onion. Cook for 5 minutes. |
| 500 ml (18 fl oz) fish or vegetable stock (see page 24)<br>100 ml (3½ fl oz) white wine | Add half the stock and the white wine. Cook for approximately 45–60 minutes, adding more liquid as needed. |
| 1 potato, peeled<br>5 ml (1 teaspoon) caraway seeds<br>freshly ground pepper | In the final 10 minutes, grate in the raw potato, and add the caraway seeds. Season with pepper, and mix well. |

**M** Virtually every country of northern continental Europe has its pickled cabbage dish. This version is Hungarian.

# PEPERONATA

**SERVES 4–6**

| | |
|---|---|
| 25 g (1 oz) unsalted butter<br>30 ml (2 tablespoons) olive oil<br>1 onion, peeled and finely sliced<br>6 large red, green and yellow peppers, seeded, cored and cut into thin strips | Sweat together in a heavy-based pan. Cover with a lid and fry until the vegetables are soft but not brown. |

8 large tomatoes,
   skinned and coarsely
   chopped
1 garlic clove, peeled
   and crushed
salt and freshly ground
   pepper
10 ml (2 teaspoons)
   caster sugar

Add, and season to taste with salt, pepper and sugar. Put the lid back on, and continue cooking over a very low heat, stirring occasionally, for about 10 minutes. The mixture should be soft, and the juices from the tomato should have evaporated.
Serve hot or cold (but not chilled).

Serve with a salad or with fish, accompanied by hot bread. This is the Italian *ratatouille*, and any left over is delicious as a sauce for pasta.

# CHERRY TOMATO COMPOTE

**SERVES 4**

30 ml (2 tablespoons)
   olive oil
3 shallots, peeled and
   finely chopped
1 garlic clove, peeled
   and finely chopped

Sweat together until soft.

450 g (1 lb) cherry
   tomatoes

Add, and sauté quickly for 3–4 minutes until the skins just start to split.

5 ml (1 teaspoon) each
   of finely cut chives
   and basil
2.5 ml (½ teaspoon)
   finely cut tarragon
salt and freshly ground
   pepper

Add, and season to taste. Serve immediately.

Serve with Potato Cakes (see page 78). The compote is also good as an accompaniment for grilled fish or the Parsnip Croquettes on page 90.

# Fennel Purée

**SERVES 4**

| | |
|---|---|
| 1 onion, peeled and finely sliced<br>1 garlic clove, peeled and crushed<br>30 ml (2 tablespoons) olive oil | Sweat together until softened. |
| 2 fennel bulbs, about 500 g (18 oz), trimmed and finely sliced | Add and cook for another 4–5 minutes. |
| 200 ml (7 fl oz) vegetable stock (see page 24) | Add and simmer gently for about 20 minutes until the fennel is very tender and the liquid has evaporated.<br>Transfer the mixture to a food processor and purée.<br>Soon the purée back into the pan. |
| salt and freshly ground pepper<br>Pernod to taste<br>25 g (1 oz) unsalted butter | Season to taste with salt and pepper, Pernod and butter. |

Fennel herb is known as *the* fish herb, and this purée of bulb fennel makes a delicious accompaniment for grilled fish dishes.

# ROASTED RED PEPPER SAUCE

### MAKES 750 ML (1¼ PINTS)
### OVEN: Moderately hot, 200°C/400°F/Gas 6

| | |
|---|---|
| 2 red peppers | Bake in the preheated oven, turning occasionally until dark spots appear on the skin, about 8 minutes. Remove from the oven, cover for 3–4 minutes, then remove the skin. Take out the core and seeds and roughly chop. |
| 1 shallot, peeled and finely chopped<br>1 garlic clove, peeled and crushed<br>15 ml (1 tablespoon) olive oil | Sweat together in a pan until softened but not browned. |
| 4 ripe tomatoes, skinned, seeded and roughly chopped | Add, mix in and cook for approximately 5 minutes until soft. |
| 120 ml (4 fl oz) vegetable stock (see page 24) | Add, along with the red pepper, and cook for another 5 minutes.<br>Transfer the mixture to a blender and purée. Return to the pan. |
| salt and freshly ground pepper | Correct seasoning and consistency (boil to reduce or add a little more stock). |
| 25 g (1 oz) unsalted butter | Whisk in, and serve or leave to cool. |

This sauce can be used instead of tomato sauce, or with pasta or gnocchi, or to accompany fish. It may be served cold or hot.

# PULSES AND GRAINS

A lthough it is little used elsewhere, the term pulses in Britain is applied to peas, beans and lentils when they are dried.

Pulses should play a major part in all our diets, as they have no fat content and contain a high level of dietary fibre. They are also very good sources of protein, especially for those who do not eat meat; this protein is 'incomplete' (ie it does not contain all the essential amino acids which form protein). Pulses should therefore be eaten in conjunction with other protein-containing nutrients and with other cereals, seeds and nuts.

Historically, pulses are important in very many cuisines through-out the world; they are satisfying, nourishing and can be eaten throughout the winter when fresh foodstuffs are scarce. They are inexpensive, flavourful, and can be used in many imaginative ways. Aduki and mung beans are eaten in the East (the latter produce Chinese beansprouts), and the various types of haricot beans – black, cannellini, flageolet and red kidney – are fundamental to cuisines as disparate as Caribbean, Italian, French and Mexican. (Haricots are perhaps even more fundamental in Britain and America, as they are *the* baked bean!)

Lentils are richer in protein than all the other pulses except for soya, and are an important staple food, particularly in India where there are many varieties, and even more dishes in which to cook them. Chickpeas are used in Middle Eastern, Greek, Spanish and North African dishes.

Grains such as wheat, corn, rye, rice etc are very valuable in the diet as well. Eaten whole or as flour, they supply fibre and, like pulses, are satisfying. *Couscous*, bulgur, semolina and wheat berries are all basic forms of wheat, and each plays a part in cuisines all over the Middle East, North Africa and Europe. *Polenta* is a dish

*Spicy chickpeas, with peas and nuts*

made from yellow cornmeal, and it is commoner than pasta in northern Italy, as is rice. This latter grain is perhaps the single most important food source in the world, supporting many cultures in Asia and the East. A good selection of varieties is now available, including *arborio* from Italy for the best *risottos*, long and short-grain from America, and the fragrant Asian *basmati*.

Buckwheat, although eaten as a grain, is actually the fruit of a plant related to sorrel and rhubarb, and is a staple in northern Europe, Asia and Russia. Cooked whole, it makes *kasha*, a pilau-like porridge; its flour is the basis of the *galette* of Brittany, the *blinis* of Russia, and the Japanese noodle called *soba*. In the UK buckwheat is often fed to pheasants, as is millet to caged birds, but millet too is a staple grain all around the world, and is useful, as is barley, in pilaffs and salads.

# Spicy Chickpeas

**SERVES 4–6**

| | |
|---|---|
| **250 g (9 oz) dried chickpeas, washed and soaked overnight** | Drain, and place in a large pot. Cover with water and simmer until tender, about 45–60 minutes. Drain and keep the liquid. |
| **1 fresh green chilli pepper, seeded**<br>**2.5 cm (1 in) fresh ginger, peeled and roughly chopped**<br>**2 garlic cloves, peeled and roughly chopped** | Grind together to a paste. |
| **30 ml (2 tablespoons) sunflower or safflower oil**<br>**1 onion, peeled and finely chopped** | Heat together and gently fry until soft. |
| **2.5 ml (½ teaspoon) cumin seeds, crushed**<br>**5 ml (1 teaspoon) coriander seeds, crushed**<br>**5 ml (1 teaspoon) chilli powder** | Add, along with the chilli paste, and fry for another minute. |
| **4 tomatoes, skinned and roughly chopped** | Add, and cook until they blend well with the onion and spices.<br>Add the drained chickpeas and cook gently for 10 minutes, adding some of their cooking liquid if needed. |
| **salt and freshly ground pepper**<br>**freshly cut coriander and mint leaves** | Season to taste, and serve, sprinkled with herb leaves. |

Add the chilli according to taste. Any leftover chickpeas is good as salad.
When fresh peas are in season, add along with some nuts.

# VEGETABLE PAELLA

**SERVES 4–6**

| | |
|---|---|
| 1 medium aubergine, trimmed and cut into 5 mm (¼ in) cubes<br>250 g (9 oz) courgettes, topped, tailed and sliced<br>salt and pepper | Place separately in colanders, lightly salt, and leave for 30 minutes. Rinse, drain and dry well. |
| 100 ml (3½ fl oz) olive oil<br>1 large onion, peeled and finely chopped<br>1 large garlic clove, peeled and crushed | Sweat together in a large frying pan for a few minutes. |
| 100 g (4 oz) carrots, peeled and cut into 1 cm (½ in) dice | Add, and cook for 2 minutes. |
| 1 red and 1 green pepper, seeded and cut into 4 cm (1½ in) strips | Add, along with the aubergines and courgettes, and cook for another 5 minutes. |
| 500 g (18 oz) long-grain rice, washed | Add, and stir to coat with oil. |
| 1.2 litres (2 pints) vegetable stock (see page 24)<br>1 packet of saffron powder<br>1 sprig of thyme<br>1 bay leaf | Add, and season with salt and pepper. Bring to the boil, cover, then simmer for 20–25 minutes until the rice is cooked and the stock absorbed. |
| 200 g (7 oz) tomato *concassée* (see page 39)<br>100 g (4 oz) peas, blanched | Add towards the end of the cooking time. Remove the thyme and bay leaf, and serve. |

# Cottage Cheese, Pineapple and Orange Millet Salad

**SERVES 4–6**

| | |
|---|---|
| 30 ml (2 tablespoons) olive oil<br>250 g (9 oz) millet | Heat together in a saucepan, stirring so that the millet is covered with the oil. Keep cooking and stirring until the millet starts to crack. |
| 750 ml (1¼ pints) vegetable stock (see page 24)<br>salt and freshly ground pepper | Pour in, season with 2.5 ml (½ teaspoon) salt, and bring to the boil. Cover and simmer for approximately 20 minutes.<br>Drain and spread the millet on a tray. Leave to cool. |
| 100 ml (3½ fl oz) olive oil<br>30 ml (2 tablespoons) lemon juice | Whisk together, seasoning with salt and pepper, then stir into the millet. |
| 100 g (4 oz) cottage cheese<br>2 celery stalks, trimmed and finely sliced<br>2 slices fresh pineapple, cut into 1 cm (½ in) chunks<br>1 orange, peeled and segmented<br>50 g (2 oz) hazelnuts, toasted and skinned<br>30 ml (2 tablespoons) finely cut chives | Add to the millet, and mix together well. Chill and serve. |

 Millet is a staple food in many parts of the East. It is also used a great deal in *pilaffs* in Russia, Poland etc.

Overleaf: *For a seafood paella, add shrimps, mussels, monkfish etc about 7–8 minutes before the end of cooking time*

# Spring Vegetable Couscous

**SERVES 4**

| | |
|---|---|
| 350 g (12 oz) couscous<br>2 litres (3½ pints) vegetable stock (see page 24) | Put couscous in a bowl and add 450 ml (15 fl oz) of the boiling stock. Leave for 10 minutes to absorb. Put the rest of the stock in a *couscoussière* or deep pot. |
| 12 button onions, peeled | Add to the stock, and bring to the boil. |
| 8 young leeks, washed and cut into 2.5 cm (1 in) batons<br>20 baby carrots, scrubbed<br>12 baby turnips, scrubbed, with 2 cm (¾ in) leafy top intact<br>2 celery stalks, cut into 2.5 cm (1 in) batons | Add to the stock in the pot.<br>Put the soaked couscous in the top half of the *couscoussière* or in a muslin-lined steamer on top of the deep pot. Set over the simmering stock, and cook for 8–10 minutes. |
| 8 baby courgettes with flowers<br>8 yellow baby squashes<br>12 cherry or small tomatoes | Remove the flowers from the courgettes. Cut the flowers into strips and add to the couscous in the top of the pot.<br>Add the courgettes, squashes and tomatoes to the stock 5 minutes before the end of cooking time. Remove and tip the couscous into a large dish, breaking up any lumps. |
| 100 g (4 oz) cooked chickpeas<br>1 packet of saffron powder<br>salt and freshly ground pepper | Add to the stock and season to taste.<br>Drain the vegetables, reserving the stock, and lay on top of the couscous. Serve the hot stock and sauce (see below) separately. |

A hot sauce is a traditional accompaniment to many couscous dishes. Mix together 5 ml (1 teaspoon) each of ground cumin and coriander, 2.5 ml (½ teaspoon) each of chilli powder and celery salt, and 15 ml (1 tablespoon) tomato purée. Dilute to taste with up to 15 ml (1 tablespoon) hot vegetable stock (see page 24).

# Courgette and Shrimp Couscous Salad

**SERVES 4–6**

| | |
|---|---|
| **250 g (9 oz) courgettes, topped and tailed** | Cut in half lengthwise, then scoop out the centre. Finely slice to end up with crescent-shaped slices. |
| **30 ml (2 tablespoons) olive oil**<br>**1 garlic clove, peeled and crushed** | Infuse together for about 1 minute over gentle heat. |
| **5 ml (1 teaspoon) curry powder**<br>**15 ml (1 tablespoon) tomato purée** | Add, and cook for another 2 minutes. |
| **350 ml (12 fl oz) vegetable stock (see page 24)** | Add, and bring to the boil. |
| **250 g (9 oz) couscous**<br>**1 red pepper, seeded and cut into thin strips** | Stir in, along with the courgettes and remove from the heat. Cover and leave to stand for approximately 5–7 minutes until the couscous has soaked up all the liquid. Fluff with a fork to separate the grains. |
| **50 ml (2 fl oz) white wine vinegar**<br>**100 ml (3½ fl oz) olive oil** | Whisk together and add to the couscous. Mix well. |
| **250 g (9 oz) peeled shrimps**<br>**30 ml (2 tablespoons) chopped parsley**<br>**salt and freshly ground pepper** | Stir in, and season to taste with salt and pepper. Leave to cool. (The salad can be served hot, in which case omit the dressing.) |

*Courgette and shrimp couscous salad*

# BULGUR WITH PEAS AND SWEETCORN

**SERVES 4**

| | |
|---|---|
| 1 small onion, peeled and finely chopped<br>15 ml (1 tablespoon) olive oil | Sweat together for a few minutes. |
| 125 g (4½ oz) bulgur | Stir in, and cook the mixture for 1 minute. |
| 200 ml (7 fl oz) vegetable stock (see page 24)<br>1 sprig of thyme | Add, and bring to the boil. Cook the mixture, covered, for approximately 5 minutes over a low heat until the bulgur absorbs most of the liquid. |
| 65 g (2½ oz) each of frozen peas and sweetcorn, defrosted and blanched<br>salt and freshly ground pepper | Add, cover, and cook for another 1–2 minutes to heat through. Season to taste with salt and pepper, then fluff and separate the grains with a fork. |

This is particularly delicious served with Spiced Aubergine and Okra Stew (see page 87).
Variously known as *bulghur, bulgar* wheat and *pourgouri bulgur* is wheat that has been 'cracked' by boiling. It is then dried and ground finely or coarsely. It is very popular in the Middle East.

# BASMATI RICE WITH SAFFRON AND BROAD BEANS

**SERVES 4**

| | |
|---|---|
| 200 g (7 oz) basmati rice<br>salt and freshly ground pepper | Wash and rinse well, then cook in a pan of boiling salted water for approximately 6–7 minutes. Drain through a sieve or colander. |

| | |
|---|---|
| 15 ml (1 tablespoon) olive oil<br>50 g (2 oz) butter<br>1 small onion, peeled and finely chopped | Sweat together for a few minutes, then add the rice and stir to mix. |
| 1 packet of saffron powder | Add, and stir to coat the rice well. |
| 250 g (9 oz) broad beans, shelled weight, blanched and skinned<br>4 pieces of Egg 'Pancake' made with herbs (see page 114), cut into strips | Add, heat through briefly and season to taste with salt and pepper. |

# HUMMUS

**MAKES 650–700 G (ABOUT 1½ LB)**

| | |
|---|---|
| 200 g (7 oz) dried chickpeas, soaked overnight | Drain, then cover generously with fresh water. Bring to the boil, and cook until the beans are completely soft, about 1–1½ hours. Drain, keeping the liquid. |
| 60 ml (4 tablespoons) *tahini*<br>2 garlic cloves, peeled and roughly chopped<br>75 ml (5 tablespoons) lemon juice<br>45 ml (3 tablespoons) virgin olive oil<br>salt and cayenne | Place in a food processor along with the chickpeas, and about 150 ml (5 fl oz) of the cooking water. Season with salt and cayenne and process until smooth. More olive oil may be added if necessary. Taste for seasoning before serving. |

Use as a dip for crudités, or spread on canapés.
*Tahini*, or sesame butter, is simply ground sesame seeds, and it is available in jars in good delicatessens. It is a thick paste, oily because of the high content of oil. (This is also extracted for use in cooking.)
If you dislike the taste of raw garlic, you could cook the cloves in a little of the chickpea liquid, before adding to the processor.

# LAYERED BUCKWHEAT CRÊPES WITH SMOKED SALMON AND CREAM CHEESE

**SERVES 4–6**

| | |
|---|---|
| 6 × 15 cm (6 in) buckwheat crêpes (see page 193) | Make according to the instructions on page 193, and leave to cool. For a neater-looking end result, trim the pancakes with a 15 cm (6 in) cutter. |
| 400 g (14 oz) cream cheese<br>2 bunches of chives, finely cut | Cream the cheese with half the chives to a soft mixture. Place in a piping bag with a small plain tube, 5 mm (½ in) in diameter. Take one pancake, lay it flat on a board, and pipe the cream cheese all the way round, starting at the centre. Smooth with a palette knife. |
| 200 g (7 oz) smoked salmon, thinly sliced | Place a slice on top of the cheese layer, and top with another pancake. Flatten slightly. Continue with this procedure four more times, finishing with a crêpe on top. With a palette knife, go round the sides, filling any gaps with cheese, and coat with the remaining cut chives. Leave in the refrigerator to firm up before cutting. |

Serve with a salad as a starter, cut in wedges, or, in smaller wedges, with drinks.
Many types of filling can be used: a mixture of blue and cream cheese; a smoked fish pâté etc.
Instead of in a cake form, you could roll individual pancakes and filling into a roulade shape, and cut into little rounds for canapés.

*Layered buckwheat crêpes with smoked salmon and cream cheese*

# POLENTA AND AUBERGINE LAYER CAKES

**SERVES 4**

**OVEN:** Moderate, 180°C/350°F/Gas 4

| | |
|---|---|
| 2 short fat aubergines, sliced into 8 × 1 cm (½ in) thick rounds<br>salt and freshly ground pepper | Place in a colander, sprinkle with salt and leave to sweat for 30–60 minutes. Then rinse the salt off, and pat the rounds dry.<br>Bring 1 litre (1¾ pints) water to the boil, and add 7.5 ml (1½ teaspoons) salt. |
| 250 g (9 oz) coarse-grained cornmeal | Whisk into the water in a stream, so there are no lumps. Lower the heat and cook slowly for about 20–25 minutes, stirring all the time.<br>When the mixture stiffens and leaves the side of the pan, it is done. Add more water if necessary. Remove from the heat. |
| 100 g (4 oz) Fontina cheese, grated<br>30 g (1¼ oz) butter<br>cayenne pepper | Add, and season with a pinch of cayenne. Mix well and pour the mixture into a greased tray in a thin layer approximately 1 cm (½ in) thick. Set aside to cool. |
| 15 ml (1 tablespoon) olive oil<br>1 shallot, peeled and finely chopped<br>1 garlic clove, peeled and finely chopped<br>1 sprig of thyme | Stew together until the onion is soft. |
| 250 g (9 oz) tomatoes, skinned, seeded and roughly diced<br>15 ml (1 tablespoon) tomato purée<br>a pinch of sugar | Stir in and cook for about 6–7 minutes until the tomato is almost a purée, but not dry. Season with salt, pepper and the sugar. |

*Polenta and aubergine layer cake*

| | |
|---|---|
| 45 ml (3 tablespoons)<br>  olive oil | Heat in a pan and fry the aubergine rounds on both sides until golden brown. Drain on kitchen paper. Cut the polenta into twelve 7.5 cm (3 in) rounds. |
| 8 basil leaves<br>15 ml (1 tablespoon)<br>  oregano leaves | To assemble the cakes, place four rounds of polenta in a row. Spread a spoonful of the tomato mixture on each piece of the polenta. Place a piece of aubergine on top, a leaf of basil and a sprinkling of oregano. Season with freshly ground pepper. Top with another round of polenta, the filling, aubergine and herb, finishing with a polenta round. Place the cakes in a greased gratin dish. |
| 75 g (3 oz) Gorgonzola<br>  cheese, crumbled<br>50 g (2 oz) Mozzarella,<br>  cut into 4 slices | Top with the cheeses, and bake in the preheated oven for about 20–25 minutes until the polenta cakes are heated right through. |

# EGG 'PANCAKE' GARNISH

### MAKES 4–6 PANCAKES

| | |
|---|---|
| 2 eggs<br>30 ml (2 tablespoons)<br>  olive oil | Beat the eggs with half the oil. |
| 15 ml (1 tablespoon)<br>  mixed fresh herbs,<br>  chopped<br>salt and freshly ground<br>  pepper | Add the herbs, and season with salt and pepper. Use the remaining oil to grease a small frying pan with a piece of cloth or kitchen paper. Heat.<br>Pour a small ladleful of the egg mixture into the frying pan and tilt the pan to distribute the egg evenly, making a 'pancake'. Cook for about 1 minute, then turn and cook the other side. Slide the 'pancake' on to a plate.<br>Cook the remaining egg mixture in this manner.<br>To cut the 'pancake' into strips, roll each into a cigar shape, then cut crosswise into fine strips. |

# Millet Pancakes with Spinach and Mozzarella

**SERVES 4**

**OVEN:** Moderately hot, 190°C/375°F/Gas 5

| | |
|---|---|
| 250 g (9 oz) millet, finely ground<br>300 ml (10 fl oz) milk<br>2 eggs, beaten<br>salt and pepper | For the pancakes, beat to a smooth dough, and leave to rest for 2 hours. |
| 300 g (11 oz) Mozzarella cheese, chopped small<br>30 ml (2 tablespoons) olive oil<br>15 g (½ oz) basil, finely cut | For the topping, mix together, and season with salt and pepper. |
| 1 shallot, peeled and finely chopped<br>25 g (1 oz) butter | For the filling, sweat together for a few minutes. |
| 400 g (14 oz) spinach leaves, washed, tough stalks removed, blanched and chopped<br>freshly grated nutmeg | Add to the shallots, and toss. Season to taste with salt, pepper and nutmeg. |
| a little butter | Heat in a pancake pan and add spoonfuls of the millet batter to make pancakes (12 large or 18 small). Spread half of each pancake with a little of the spinach filling. Place the cheese topping on top, and then fold over the other half of the pancake.<br>Place on a baking sheet and warm through in the preheated oven for about 20 minutes. |

If you like, serve with a sauce like the Roasted Red Pepper Sauce on page 97. Two pancakes could be enough for one portion: freeze the remainder.
Grind the millet in a (clean) coffee mill.

# BLINIS

## MAKES ABOUT 24

| | |
|---|---|
| **15 g (½ oz) fresh yeast**<br>**a pinch of caster sugar**<br>**250 ml (8 fl oz)**<br>  **lukewarm milk** | Cream together. |
| **100 g (4 oz) plain flour** | Place in a bowl and beat in the yeast mixture. Leave in a warm place to prove, about 30–60 minutes. |
| **3 egg yolks**<br>**150 g (5 oz) buckwheat**<br>  **flour** | Mix in, and leave to prove again for another 30 minutes. |
| **3 egg whites**<br>**a pinch of salt** | Whisk together until stiff. Fold into the batter. |
| **butter** | Heat a little in a frying pan.<br>Drop a tablespoonful of the batter into the frying pan. Cook about three or four at a time. Cook for 2–3 minutes until bubbles start to appear, the edges start to set and the underside is light brown in colour. Turn over and cook on the other side, another 2 or so minutes.<br>Leave to cool, covered with a cloth. |

**M** Blinis, a Russian speciality, are usually served with caviar and soured cream. You could also top them with coarsely chopped hard-boiled egg and smoked salmon, or soured cream with chopped celery and a few wheat sprouts (see page 138). Make bite-sized blinis for canapés.

# GRILLED TOFU WITH MISO TOPPING

**SERVES 4**

| | |
|---|---|
| 100 g (4 oz) red *miso*<br>50 g (2 oz) white *miso*<br>2 egg yolks<br>30 ml (2 tablespoons) each of *saké* and *mirin*<br>30 ml (2 tablespoons) caster sugar | Combine in the top of a double boiler. Place over bottom boiler holding some boiling water. |
| 105 ml (7 tablespoons) vegetable stock (see page 24) | Stir into the *miso*, and mix until it thickens. |
| 250 g (9 oz) fresh cotton *tofu* | Remove from its water, and wrap in a clean cloth. Press with a plate and stand for about an hour (to remove excess water). Cut the *tofu* into small rectangular pieces.<br>Grill or pan-fry for about 2–3 minutes until speckled brown all over.<br>Spread with the *miso* topping. |
| sesame seeds | Garnish with sesame seeds. |

Serve on its own, or with a stir-fry of your favourite vegetables. *Tofu* can be charcoal-grilled for even better flavour. Skewer each piece with two short bamboo skewers; it is very fragile and should be handled with care.

# YOGHURT WITH BERRIES AND MILLET

**SERVES 4–6**

| | |
|---|---|
| **150 g (5 oz) millet** | Soak in water overnight, then cook in a pressure cooker for 10 minutes. (Or simply cook in water for 20–25 minutes on top of the stove.) Allow to cool. |
| **50 g (2 oz) pine kernels** | Toast in a non-stick pan without fat, then cool. |
| **400 g (14 oz) natural yoghurt**<br>**200 g (7 oz) mixed berries**<br>**15 ml (1 tablespoon) chopped mint**<br>**60 ml (4 tablespoons) honey, or to taste** | Mix the yoghurt with the millet, three-quarters of the berries, and some of the mint. Sweeten with honey to taste.<br>Arrange on plates, and decorate with the remaining berries and mint. Sprinkle with the toasted pine kernels. |

# Muesli with Exotic Fruits

**SERVES 8**

| | |
|---|---|
| **100 g (4 oz) whole wheat berries** | Soak for several hours, or overnight, then cook in a pressure cooker for 15–20 minutes. (Or cook in water on top of the stove for at least an hour.) Cool. |
| **1 mango**<br>**½ large pineapple**<br>**1 papaya** | Peel and stone, seed and core as appropriate. Cut the flesh into cubes. |
| **2 passion fruit** | Cut in half and scrape the fleshy seeds out into a dish. |
| **250 ml (8 fl oz) milk**<br>**30 ml (2 tablespoons) honey** | Mix into the passion fruit along with the cooled wheat berries. Fold in the other fruits and arrange on plates. Serve some more milk or cream separately. |

# PASTA

Although pasta is indissolubly liked in most people's minds with Italy, the basic flour and water – and occasionally egg – mixture which forms noodles and other pasta shapes is a feature of many more cuisines than just the Italian. In Italy, America and the UK, the flour used for pasta is strong or durum wheat, plain or wholegrain, but in China for instance, rice is used, in Japan, buckwheat, and in other parts of the East a mung-bean or chickpea flour. In Hungary, small pellets called *tarhonya* or 'egg barley' are made from wheat flour, egg and water, and the German *nudeln* and *spätzle* are well known. However, it is still in Italy that pasta reigns supreme.

A helping of pasta in Italy, as in most other countries where it is found, is served as a sauce accompaniment as a separate dish, or instead of vegetables. In Central Europe pasta is more often the substance of everyday meat-less cooking, combined with eggs, cheese or vegetables. The combination of a good sauce and pasta is a healthy one, providing a nutritionally well-balanced meal; and pastas made from gram, cornmeal or wholewheat flours add protein, fibre and some vitamins as well as carbohydrate. (The night before the London marathon race, runners are encouraged to eat meals of pasta, proof positive of its sustaining and energy-giving powers!)

Pastas are available dried or fresh, and although fresh pasta is delicious and enormously satisfying to make – and can be flavoured and coloured in so many ways (see page 122) – bought dried pasta is usually very good. Always cook any kind of pasta in lots of boiling salted water so that it has no chance to stick together; a little oil helps as well. Cook only until the pasta is *al dente*, when it still has some give to the bite, never until soft; fresh home-made pasta takes moments only.

A basic home-made pasta dough can be cut into long noodles,

*Egg noodle salad with aubergine and
mangetouts*

thick, thin or broad, or stuffed as *ravioli* and *tortellini*. (Stuffed pastas are found elsewhere – the *won ton* of China and the buckwheat *pierogi* of Poland etc.)

The sauces and fillings are what make pasta interesting, and even without meat, there is plenty of choice. For Italian pasta dishes, often olive oil with garlic and some herbs is all that is needed; and the tomato sauces here or on page 39 are deliciously fresh. The pesto and red pepper sauces on pages 89 and 97 are good too.

*Gnocchi* are not strictly a pasta – more a dumpling – but they are another product of Italy. Here they are made from potato and spinach, but they can also be made with pumpkin, and of leftover *polenta* (see page 112). They too provide a good source of carbohydrate, and can be served with different sauces.

# WHOLEMEAL PASTA

**MAKES 800 G (1¾ LB)**

**400 g (14 oz) fine
wholemeal flour
100 g (4 oz) semolina
5 eggs, beaten
15 ml (1 tablespoon)
salt
30 ml (2 tablespoons)
olive oil**

Knead together to an elastic dough. If it is still sticky, add a little more flour, or semolina, by sprinkling it on the work surface.

Form the dough into balls, wrap in foil, and allow to rest for 2 hours, somewhere not too cool.

Finally, either by means of a rolling pin or a pasta machine, roll the dough out very thinly. If using a machine, gradually narrow the blades.

Cut the dough into the shapes required.

Cook the pasta in a lot of salted water with a few drops of oil. The pasta is ready when it starts to rise to the surface – a few minutes only.

Pour into a colander and rinse in cold water. Then toss in butter or oil, or serve with a sauce.

## TOMATO PASTA
Work in 30 ml (2 tablespoons) tomato purée.

## MUSHROOM PASTA
Mince 20 g (¾ oz) dried and reconstituted mushrooms very finely and then knead in.

## SPINACH PASTA
Mix 100 g (4 oz) blanched and very well drained spinach purée with the eggs.

## HERB PASTA
Mix 50 g (2 oz) fresh herbs (mixed if desired) with the eggs before making the dough.
Particularly tasty are sorrel noodles and basil noodles.

## SAFFRON PASTA
Beat 2 packets of saffron powder (each pack contains 0.125 g, so 25 g/1 oz) into the eggs.

## BLACK INK PASTA
Add at least 10 packets of squid ink to the dough.

## BUCKWHEAT PASTA
Substitute half of the wholemeal flour with buckwheat flour.

# EGG NOODLE SALAD WITH AUBERGINE AND MANGETOUTS

**SERVES 4–6**

30 ml (2 tablespoons)
sherry vinegar
20 ml (4 teaspoons)
balsamic vinegar
5 ml (1 teaspoon) caster
sugar
100 ml (3½ fl oz) light
soy sauce
60 ml (4 tablespoons)
sesame oil
40 ml (1½ fl oz) light
olive oil
2 red chilli peppers,
seeded and finely cut
salt and freshly ground
pepper

Mix together for the dressing, and season with a little salt and pepper.

---

1 garlic clove, peeled
2 slices fresh ginger,
peeled

Chop together very finely.

---

30 ml (2 tablespoons)
olive oil
200 g (7 oz) long thin
aubergines, cut into
slices then into fine
strips

Heat half of the olive oil in a pan and add half the garlic and ginger mixture and the aubergines. Cook until soft, then transfer to a large bowl.

---

200 g (7 oz)
beansprouts, washed
and dried

Cook briefly in the remaining oil, with the remaining garlic and ginger. Add to the aubergines.

---

400 g (14 oz) fresh fine
Chinese egg noodles

Cook in a large pan of boiling water. Stir to separate. This takes only a few minutes – be careful not to overcook. Put into a colander and rinse in cold water. Shake off any excess liquid and place in the bowl with the aubergine and beansprouts.
Pour in the dressing, except for a few tablespoonfuls.

---

| | |
|---|---|
| 25 g (1 oz) fresh coriander, roughly cut<br>1 bunch spring onions, finely cut | Add, and toss the noodle mixture well together. Take a large fork and wind the noodles around it. Mound these on to individual plates. |

| | |
|---|---|
| 100 g (4 oz) mangetouts<br>50 g (2 oz) carrots, scrubbed<br>30 ml (2 tablespoons) sesame seeds, toasted | String the mangetouts, cut into fine strips and blanch. Cut the carrots into long fine strips. Season separately with salt, pepper and the remaining dressing. Scatter on top of the noodles. Garnish with sesame seeds. |

# BUCKWHEAT NOODLES WITH AVOCADO

### SERVES 4

| | |
|---|---|
| 200 g (7 oz) dried buckwheat noodles<br>salt and pepper | Cook in a pan of boiling salted water with a dash of oil for approximately 5–7 minutes, keeping them *al dente*. Drain well and set aside. |

| | |
|---|---|
| 25 g (1 oz) butter<br>30 ml (2 tablespoons) olive oil<br>2 garlic cloves, peeled and finely chopped<br>2 shallots, peeled and finely chopped<br>25 g (1 oz) sun-dried tomato in oil, cut into fine strips | Heat together in a large frying pan for a few minutes. |

| | |
|---|---|
| 2 firm ripe avocadoes<br>15 ml (1 tablespoon) chopped parsley<br>15 g (½ oz) basil leaves, cut into strips<br>25 g (1 oz) Parmesan cheese, grated | Peel, stone, and cut avocado flesh into medium dice. Add all along with the noodles, and season with salt and pepper. Toss gently until all the ingredients are heated through.<br>Serve accompanied by extra grated Parmesan cheese. |

Instead of the above ingredients, you could toss the noodles with strips of smoked salmon, crumbled grated cheese and rocket or arugula leaves as in the photograph.

*Buckwheat noodles with avocado*

# RAVIOLI WITH FETA CHEESE AND SPINACH

**SERVES 4–6**

| | |
|---|---|
| 30 ml (2 tablespoons) olive oil<br>1 garlic clove, peeled and finely chopped<br>65 g (2½ oz) shallots, peeled and chopped | Sweat together for 2–3 minutes without colouring. Remove from the heat. |
| 150 (5 oz) young leaf spinach, blanched<br>200 g (7 oz) Feta cheese, crumbled | Place with the shallot mixture into a food processor and process finely. |
| 50 g (2 oz) Parmesan cheese, finely grated<br>salt and pepper | Add, and correct seasoning with salt and pepper. |
| 300 g (11 oz) pasta dough (see page 122), any flavour | For the ravioli, divide in two, then roll both pieces thinly to roughly the same size (or use the pasta machine). |
| 1 egg, beaten | Brush some over one-half of the pasta dough, and mark lightly with a round 8 cm (3¼ in) cutter.<br>Pipe or put about 5 ml (1 teaspoon) of the filling on to each lightly etched circle. Lay the second piece of the pasta dough on top and press lightly.<br>Cut through both layers of dough, around the mounds of filling, to make and separate the ravioli. Press the edges together well to seal.<br>Cook the ravioli to *al dente* in a large pan of boiling salted water, about 4–5 minutes. |
| 1 quantity Pesto, made with basil (see page 89)<br>15 ml (1 tablespoon) whipping cream | Heat gently together in a pan, then add the ravioli, turning gently for a minute or two.<br>Divide the ravioli between individual heatproof plates with some of the sauce. |

**finely grated Sbrinz
cheese**
**toasted pine kernels**
**tomato** *concassée* **(see
page 39)**

Garnish with a sprinkle of cheese, toasted pine
kernels and tomato, then flash under a hot grill.
Serve immediately.

Any number of fillings and sauces can be used for raviolis. Try
the goat cheese filling below, or any of the sauces elsewhere in
the book.

# GOAT CHEESE FILLING
# FOR PASTA

### MAKES ABOUT 400 G (14 OZ)

**1 large shallot, peeled
and finely chopped**
**30 ml (2 tablespoons)
olive oil**
**1 small garlic clove,
peeled and crushed**
**100 g (4 oz) leek,
washed and finely
diced**

Sweat together until the vegetables are soft. Remove
from the heat and cool.

**200 g (7 oz)** *taupinière*
**goat cheese**

Beat until smooth.

**100 g (4 oz)** *fromage
blanc*, **drained**
**1 egg, beaten**

Combine with the beaten goat cheese, and add to the
cooked shallot mixture.

**15 ml (1 tablespoon)
finely chopped
parsley**
**salt and freshly ground
pepper**
**cayenne pepper**
**freshly grated nutmeg**

Mix in, and season to taste with salt, pepper, cayenne
and nutmeg.

This is a good filling for ravioli. You could add spinach purée to
the mixture to make it more substantial as a cannelloni filling.

# SPINACH GNOCCHI WITH PEPPER AND CHEESE SAUCES

**SERVES 4**

**OVEN:** Moderately hot, 190°C/375°F/Gas 5

| | |
|---|---|
| 500 g (18 oz) potatoes, scrubbed | Bake in their jackets in the preheated oven. Remove the flesh from the skin and pass through a sieve. |
| 100 g (4 oz) plain flour<br>1 egg<br>1 egg yolk<br>50 g (2 oz) spinach purée, dried well<br>salt and freshly ground pepper<br>freshly grated nutmeg | Mix in while the potato is hot. Season to taste with salt, pepper and nutmeg.<br>Spoon the mixture into a piping bag with a 2 cm (¾ in) plain nozzle. Pipe the mixture out into lengths on a floured board or work surface. Cut into little logs of 3–4 cm (1¼–1½ in) in length. Dust well with extra flour and roll each piece in your hands. Press with a fork to flatten slightly and give it a pattern, and place the gnocchi in a floured tray.<br>Poach in gently boiling water for approximately 5 minutes, then remove with a slotted spoon and drain carefully. |
| 400 ml (14 fl oz) Roasted Red Pepper Sauce (see page 97) | Heat and pour into a suitably sized earthenware dish. Arrange the gnocchi on top. |
| 100 ml (3½ fl oz) Blue Cheese Sauce (see page 165) | Pour over the gnocchi, and gratinate under a hot grill or in the oven until hot and bubbling. Serve immediately. |

Once you have your basic gnocchi, you can serve them in a variety of ways. Another of my favourites is to heat up the gnocchi with some butter infused with sage leaves, a few pitted, oil-cured black olives, and some grated Parmesan (see page 2).

*Spinach gnocchi with pepper and cheese sauces*

# LASAGNE WITH MOZZARELLA

**SERVES 8**

**OVEN:** Moderately hot, 200°C/400°F/Gas 6

450 g (1 lb) Ricotta
  cheese, sieved
225 g (8 oz) Mozzarella
  cheese, diced
2 shallots, peeled and
  finely chopped
20 g (¾ oz) finely cut
  basil, oregano and
  parsley
450 g (1 lb) tomatoes,
  skinned and diced
salt and freshly ground
  pepper

For the filling, mix together well, then season with salt and pepper.

---

1 small onion, peeled
  and finely chopped
1 carrot, peeled and
  chopped
1 celery stalk, peeled
  and chopped
2 garlic cloves, peeled
  and chopped
30 ml (2 tablespoons)
  sunflower oil

For the sauce, sweat together for a few minutes.

---

15 g (½ oz) basil, finely
  cut
1 small bay leaf
750 g (1½ lb) tomatoes,
  coarsely chopped
15 ml (1 tablespoon)
  tomato purée
120 ml (4 fl oz) white
  wine
120 ml (4 fl oz) double
  cream

Add to the sauce along with some salt and pepper, and simmer for 15 minutes.
Remove the bay leaf. Purée the sauce in a blender and push through a sieve.

---

65 g (2½ oz) Parmesan
  cheese, grated

Work 40 g (1½ oz) of the cheese into the sauce.

---

| ½ quantity Wholemeal Pasta dough (see page 122), rolled and cut into rectangles | Cook in salted water until *al dente*, then rinse in cold water and allow to cool. Drain thoroughly. |
| --- | --- |
| 15 g (½ oz) butter | Use to grease an ovenproof dish, then put in a layer of pasta (one-third), spread with half the Ricotta filling mixture, and cover with about half of the tomato sauce.<br>Continue making layers in this way until all the ingredients have been used. Finish with the remaining tomato sauce, and sprinkle with the remaining Parmesan.<br>Bake in the preheated oven for 45 minutes. To serve, cut the layered lasagne into rectangles. |

 You could vary the filling. Use a combination of cheese, tomatoes and spinach with the same tomato sauce, or a mushroom goulash (see page 84) and a cream sauce bound with egg yolk.

# STIR-FRY BLACK NOODLES WITH SQUID

**SERVES 4**

| | |
|---|---|
| **10 ml (2 teaspoons) fermented black beans, rinsed**<br>**1 slice fresh ginger, peeled**<br>**1 garlic clove, peeled** | Grind together in a mortar with a pestle to make a black bean paste. |
| **30 ml (2 tablespoons) vegetable oil** | Heat in a wok. |
| **500 g (18 oz) baby squid, cleaned** | Stir in, and cook for 2 minutes. |
| **100 g (4 oz) mussels, cooked**<br>**2 spring onions, finely sliced**<br>**1 chilli pepper, seeded and finely sliced**<br>**2 tomatoes, skinned, seeded and diced** | Add to the wok along with the black bean paste, and stir well to mix. |
| **300 g (11 oz) home-made black ink noodles, blanched (see page 122)** | Toss in, and mix well, adding more oil if needed. Continue to toss and turn until the noodles are hot. |
| **30 ml (2 tablespoons) fresh coriander leaves** | Add, and serve immediately. |

*Stir-fry black noodles with squid*

# Saffron Angel Hair with Aubergine and Sweet Pepper

**SERVES 4**

| | |
|---|---|
| 1 aubergine, cut into 1 cm (½ in) cubes<br>salt and freshly ground pepper | Place in a colander, sprinkle with salt, and leave to sweat for 30 minutes. Rinse, drain and pat dry. |
| 30 ml (2 tablespoons) olive oil<br>1 garlic clove, peeled and crushed | Heat together in a large frying pan along with the aubergine cubes, and cook until the cubes are soft and golden in colour. |
| 1 yellow and 1 red pepper, roasted (see page 97), skinned and cut into 1 cm (½ in) cubes<br>225 g (8 oz) canned plum tomatoes and liquid, passed through a sieve | Add, and bring to the boil. |
| 15 g (½ oz) basil leaves, cut into strips<br>50 g (2 oz) rocket, torn into bite-sized pieces | Add. |
| 250 g (9 oz) thin saffron noodles (see page 122) | Cook in plenty of salted boiling water, then drain well and transfer straight to the pan with the sauce. Mix and correct seasoning.<br>Take a roasting or large fork, and twirl or twist a portion of noodles around the fork. Place on individual plates with some sauce. |
| freshly grated Parmesan cheese | Serve in a bowl to be sprinkled over the portions. |

# TOMATO, OLIVE AND BASIL SAUCE

**SERVES 4–6**

1 onion, peeled and chopped
1 garlic clove, peeled and crushed
60 ml (4 tablespoons) olive oil

Sweat together for a few minutes.

---

15 g (½ oz) basil, leaves and stalks, coarsely chopped

Add, and sweat for a few seconds.

---

500 g (18 oz) fresh tomatoes, quartered
30 ml (2 tablespoons) tomato purée
120 ml (4 fl oz) dry white wine
3 anchovy fillets, finely chopped
salt and freshly ground pepper

Add, mix and season with salt and pepper.
Allow the sauce to simmer for 10 minutes, then press through a sieve (but not too fine a mesh).

---

100 g (4 oz) black olives, stoned and quartered
15 g (½ oz) basil leaves, cut into thin strips

Add, and roughly mix in.

---

Serve warm with pasta dishes, or warm or cold with fried fish.

# SALADS AND DRESSINGS

I could quite happily live on salads. Raw salads, amalgams of leaves of all shapes, colours and flavours, often with vegetables such as tomatoes and cucumbers, are good for everyone, for raw foods are more nutritious than cooked. They contain vitamins, minerals and fibre, and are low in fat. The nature of salads however, has developed over the years. Now vegetables normally used in other ways can be mixed into a colourful salad combination: avocado, fennel, courgette, broccoli or cauliflower, small turnips or kohlrabi. Used raw, plus vitamin-rich sprouted seeds or grains (see page 138), they add a great deal to the nutritive content of a salad, as can cooked grains and pulses, selected fruits, nuts, seeds and protein foods such as cheese or fish. Garnishing additions such as croûtons can add flavour and texture as well as bulk.

The key to success for most salads is the dressing, though, and there is much more of a choice than just a mixture of oil and vinegar. Always use the best red and white wine vinegars, sherry and champagne vinegars are also available, as is the Italian balsamic. You can also make your own flavoured vinegars: do so either from scratch using a mother of vinegar (available in health-food shops) or by putting a flavouring into good wine vinegar (macerate together for a couple of weeks in a dark place). For the latter, flavour red, for instance, with rosemary, thyme or raspberries; white with tarragon, shallots or garlic. I also make a lime vinegar, using the flesh and strips of peel.

I choose my vinegars according to the leaves I am dressing. I use a mild soft one such as champagne or white wine with tender and delicate lettuce leaves; a stronger one such as an aged red wine or sherry vinegar with sturdier green leaves like Cos or spinach (I would also use a heavier, fruitier oil); and balsamic vinegar plus

*Plum tomatoes with sprouts*

nut oils and other ingredients such as mustard and cream with the chicories.

Oils used in salad dressings are just as important. Cold pressed virgin olive oils are delicious and healthy, and the nut oils add their unique scents. You can also flavour oils in much the same way as you can vinegars. Fill a jar with olive oil and a favourite herb, and let stand in a cool dark place for a couple of weeks; mixed peppercorns and dried chilli peppers could be marinated similarly for a chilli oil; or about 6 cloves of garlic (and herbs) for a garlic (or garlic herb) oil. These can obviously be used in dressings, but are also delicious with pizzas, pastas and vegetable dishes.

Many cheeses can make successful dressings for salads (see pages 70 and 164), and *tofu*, the soya curd of the Japanese, makes a healthier alternative to mayonnaise.

# PLUM TOMATOES WITH SPROUTS

**SERVES 4**

| | |
|---|---|
| **8 fresh plum tomatoes**<br>**salt and pepper** | Thinly slice, place on a tray, and season with salt and pepper. |
| **7.5 ml (1½ teaspoons)**<br>**sherry vinegar**<br>**15 ml (1 tablespoon)**<br>**balsamic vinegar**<br>**25 ml (1 fl oz) each of**<br>**olive and walnut oils** | Mix together, adding a little salt and pepper, and use a little to moisten the tomatoes. |
| **1 celery stick**<br>**1 small carrot, peeled**<br>**1 small firm, ripe**<br>**avocado, peeled**<br>**25 g (1 oz) each of**<br>**alfalfa sprouts and**<br>**wheat sprouts**<br>**15 ml (1 tablespoon)**<br>**finely sliced spring**<br>**onion** | Cut celery and carrot into fine strips of 2.5 cm (1 in) long. Cut the avocado flesh into 1 cm (½ in) dice. Rinse and drain the sprouts.<br>Combine together in a large bowl, and season with salt, pepper and a little of the dressing.<br>Arrange the tomato slices on individual plates, overlapping slightly to form a circle. |
| **100 g (4 oz) cottage**<br>**cheese**<br>  Feta<br>  Halomini . | Divide between the plates, placing it in the centre of the tomato, and top with the avocado and sprout mixture, making a nice neat mound. |
| **15 ml (1 tablespoon)**<br>**finely cut coriander** | Moisten the tomato with more dressing when necessary and sprinkle with coriander. |

For sprouts, simply put a handful of your chosen seed, grain or pulse into a large glass jar, cover with lukewarm water and leave for about 12 hours. Cover the jar with a piece of muslin and attach with an elastic band. Pour the water from the jar through the cloth, and then put the jar in a dark dry place for the germination to begin. Rinse the seeds once or twice a day with lukewarm water, draining them well, and in 3–6 days, depending on the type, you will have sprouts of varying lengths.

# BLACK BEAN, TOMATO AND CORN SALAD

**SERVES 4–6**

| | |
|---|---|
| **250 g (9 oz) black beans, soaked overnight** | Drain, then re-cover with plenty of water. |
| **1 onion, peeled and studded with 2 cloves**<br>**1 bay leaf**<br>**1 sprig of thyme** | Add, bring to a simmer and cook for approximately 45–60 minutes until the beans are tender but not mushy. Drain and remove the onion and herbs. |
| **250 g (9 oz) corn kernels, cut from 3 corn on the cobs**<br>**a little vegetable oil**<br>**salt and freshly ground pepper** | Cook in a little water with a splash of oil and a pinch of salt for 5–6 minutes. Drain. |
| **100 g (4 oz) tomato *concassée* (see page 39)**<br>**1 bunch of spring onions, finely chopped**<br>**25 g (1 oz) fresh coriander leaves, roughly chopped** | Combine with the beans and corn kernels in a large bowl. |
| **15 ml (1 tablespoon) white wine vinegar**<br>**juice of ½ lemon**<br>**5 ml (1 teaspoon) ground cumin**<br>**150 ml (5 fl oz) olive oil** | Mix together, season with a little salt and pepper, then pour over the salad. Leave to cool. |

Perhaps this should be called Mosimann's Salad, as it utilises our colours, black, red and yellow!

# BROCCOLI AND CAULIFLOWER SALAD

**SERVES 4**

250 g (9 oz) each of
  broccoli and
  cauliflower florets
salt and freshly ground
  pepper

Blanch separately in boiled salted water, then refresh in cold water. Drain well.

---

50 g (2 oz) hazelnuts,
  lightly roasted, skins
  removed, then
  coarsely ground
15 ml (1 tablespoon)
  white wine vinegar
15 ml (1 tablespoon)
  light soy sauce
5 ml (1 teaspoon) chilli
  oil (see page 137)
30 ml (2 tablespoons)
  hazelnut oil
5 ml (1 teaspoon) caster
  sugar

Mix together and season to taste with salt and pepper.
Add the cauliflower and broccoli florets to the dressing, and toss well.

---

a few hazelnuts, toasted
2 red chilli peppers,
  seeded and cut into
  fine strips

Garnish with the hazelnuts and strips of chilli.

From top: *Black bean, tomato and corn salad, and Broccoli and cauliflower salad*

# Cos Lettuce with Red Lentils in Ginger Cream

**SERVES 4**

| | |
|---|---|
| **150 g (5 oz) red lentils,**<br>**salt and freshly ground**<br>**pepper** | Cook in boiling salted water until just tender, about 10 minutes. Drain and rinse in cold water, then drain well again. |
| **30 ml (2 tablespoons)**<br>**apple juice**<br>**10 g (¼ oz) fresh**<br>**ginger, grated**<br>**60 ml (4 tablespoons)**<br>**walnut oil**<br>**30 ml (2 tablespoons)**<br>**fruit vinegar** | Mix together for the dressing. |
| **2 Cos lettuces, washed,**<br>**and divided into**<br>**leaves**<br>**8 small spring onions,**<br>**with green tops,**<br>**halved, lengthwise** | Place in a bowl and dress with half the dressing. |
| **120 ml (4 fl oz) double**<br>**cream** | Mix into the remaining dressing and pour over the lentils.<br>Arrange the leaves and onions in a star shape on a dish, and place the lentils in the middle. |
| **2 red apples, cored and**<br>**sliced**<br>**80 g (3¼ oz) walnuts,**<br>**chopped**<br>**lemon balm leaves** | Place the sliced apples and chopped walnuts on top of the lentils, and garnish with the lemon balm leaves. |

Romaine (or Romano), a sweeter variety of Cos lettuce, is sometimes available, and is good used in this recipe.

# PEARL BARLEY SALAD

**SERVES 4**

| | |
|---|---|
| 15 ml (1 tablespoon) olive oil<br>200 g (7 oz) pearl barley | Heat together in a pan, and stir to coat the barley well with the oil. |
| 500 ml (18 fl oz) vegetable stock (see page 24)<br>a pinch of saffron strands (optional) | Add, bring to the boil, and simmer for 30–40 minutes until the barley is tender, adding more liquid if necessary. Drain off the liquid and turn the barley into a bowl. |
| juice of 2 lemons<br>75 ml (5 tablespoons) olive oil<br>salt and freshly ground pepper | Mix together, and season with a little salt and pepper.<br>Stir this into the pearl barley and allow to cool. |
| ½ cucumber, peeled, seeded and cut into 5 mm (¼ in) dice<br>4 pieces sun-dried tomato in oil, cut into 5 mm (¼ in) dice<br>12 black olives, pitted and quartered<br>1 red chilli, seeded and finely sliced<br>30 ml (2 tablespoons) each of finely cut mint and coriander | Mix into the pearl barley, and taste for seasoning. |

You could use cracked wheat instead of the pearl barley. Once the stock has come to the boil, remove from the heat and let it soak for 7–10 minutes until the wheat is soft. Drain and proceed as above.
You could use pot barley (the unhusked barley grain) instead of pearl; it takes a little longer to cook. It can benefit from being soaked beforehand.

# Melon, Cucumber and Tomato Salad with Mint

**SERVES 4–6**

**1 cucumber**
**salt and freshly ground**
**pepper**

Peel, cut in half lengthwise, scoop out the seeds and slice across into crescents approximately 5 mm (¼ in) thick. Place in a colander and sprinkle with a little salt. Leave for 15–20 minutes to drain out some of the juices. Thoroughly rinse and press dry.

**1 cantaloupe melon**
**1 charentais or ogen**
**melon**
**¼ small red**
**watermelon**

Meanwhile, cut in halves, remove the seeds and make into balls using a parisian scoop. Be careful to remove all the watermelon seeds. (Trimmings from the melons can be kept and puréed for a cold soup.)

**100 g (4 oz) red cherry**
**tomatoes**
**100 g (4 oz) yellow pear**
**tomatoes**
**30 ml (2 tablespoons)**
**finely cut mint**

Combine with the cucumber and melon balls in a large bowl.

**7.5 ml (1½ teaspoons)**
**clear honey**
**15 ml (1 tablespoon)**
**balsamic vinegar**
**7.5 ml (1½ teaspoons)**
**orange juice**
**45 ml (3 tablespoons)**
**olive oil**

Mix together, seasoning with a little salt and pepper, and use to dress the salad. Toss and serve.

Yellow pear tomatoes are tiny, like cherry tomatoes, and very tasty.

*Melon, cucumber and tomato salad with mint,*
*garnished with nasturtiums*

# AVOCADO AND ORANGE SUNFLOWER SALAD

**SERVES 4**

| | |
|---|---|
| 3 sweet oranges | Peel and segment. Squeeze out the juice from the pulp. |
| juice of 1 lime<br>85 ml (3 fl oz) olive oil<br>5 ml (1 teaspoon) clear honey<br>salt and freshly ground pepper | Mix with the orange juice, and season with salt and pepper. |
| 2 ripe avocadoes, peeled, stoned and sliced | Season with a little salt and moisten with some of the dressing.<br>Arrange the avocado slices like flower petals on individual plates, place the orange segments in the middle, and drizzle with a little dressing. |
| 12 mint leaves, cut into fine strips<br>50 g (2 oz) sunflower seeds, toasted | Top with mint strips, and scatter with sunflower seeds. |

To toast sunflower seeds, simply place them on a piece of foil under the grill and toast for a few minutes until they pop and brown. (Or place them in a moderate oven for a few minutes.) Pine kernels and pumpkin seeds can be toasted in the same way.

# Spinach Salad with Goat's Cheese

**SERVES 4**

| | |
|---|---|
| 10 ml (2 teaspoons) lemon juice<br>5 ml (1 teaspoon) strong mustard<br>200 g (7 oz) low-fat natural yoghurt<br>40 g (1½ oz) goat's cheese, crushed with a fork<br>salt and freshly ground pepper | For the dressing, mix together well, and season to taste with salt and pepper. |
| 250 g (9 oz) fresh young spinach, tough stalks removed | Wash well, then drain and dry on a towel. Place in a bowl. |
| 1 red pepper, roasted and skinned (see page 97) | Remove all the cores and seeds, and cut the flesh into fine strips. Add to the spinach.<br>Pour the dressing over the spinach and pepper, and mix in well. |
| 75 g (3 oz) wholemeal garlic croûtons (see page 25)<br>15 g (½ oz) parsley, chopped<br>5 g (¼ oz) basil, finely cut | Sprinkle over the salad, and serve immediately, otherwise the spinach will wilt. |

 Fresh raw spinach is delicious, but lettuce, curly endive, or radicchio – any fairly sturdy salad leaf – may be used instead.

Overleaf: *Carpaccio of kohlrabi with blue cheese dressing*

# Carpaccio of Kohlrabi with Blue Cheese Dressing

**SERVES 4**

| | |
|---|---|
| **2 kohlrabi, approx. 550–600 g (1¼ lb) in weight** | Peel with a small knife, and cut into paper-thin slices using a mandoline. Place in a bowl. |
| **1 quantity Blue Cheese Dressing (see page 164)** <br> **salt and freshly ground pepper** | Pour over the kohlrabi slices, and toss well. Season to taste with salt and pepper if necessary. <br> Arrange the kohlrabi slices on individual plates, some flat and some folded, to give the dish 'life'. |
| **about 50 g (2 oz) blue cheese, crumbled** <br> **4 radishes, finely sliced** <br> **30 ml (2 tablespoons) finely cut chives** | Sprinkle over the plates. You could leave the chives whole as in the photograph. |

 Kohlrabi is a member of the cabbage family, although it looks a little like a turnip. It has a vaguely peppery flavour like raw turnip, and is a popular vegetable in Central Europe. It can be served raw – grated in many traditional recipes – or boiled or baked. It can be stuffed and baked with soured cream, and accompanies the main meat course for special occasions in Hungary.

# Tofu Mayonnaise

**MAKES 150–200 ML (5–7 FL OZ)**

| | |
|---|---|
| **100 g (4 oz) *tofu*** <br> **5 ml (1 teaspoon) Dijon mustard** <br> **15 ml (1 tablespoon) lemon juice** | Blend together in a food processor until well blended. |
| **50 ml (2 fl oz) olive oil** | Trickle in in a stream, then blend the mayonnaise until it emulsifies. |

| a little vegetable stock (see page 24) salt and freshly ground pepper | Thin down with stock if necessary, and taste to correct seasoning. |

---

 If the mixture starts to separate, add 15 ml (1 tablespoon) boiling water.
Any herbs such as chives, tarragon or basil can be added, or soy sauce, or diced sweet peppers.
*Tofu* is a curd 'cheese' made from soya-bean milk, known as *tofu* in Japan, but of Chinese origin. It has little taste of its own, but is rich in nutrients, and makes a much healthier mayonnaise than one containing egg yolks.

# CAESAR DRESSING

**SERVES 8**

| 1 small garlic clove, peeled 2 egg yolks 2 anchovies 100 ml (3½ fl oz) sherry vinegar 40 g (1½ oz) Parmesan cheese, freshly grated | Place in a blender, and blend until smooth and creamy. |

---

| 200 ml (7 fl oz) olive oil 100 ml (3½ fl oz) vegetable stock (see page 24) | Trickle in the oil and thin down to taste with the stock. |

---

| salt and freshly ground pepper a drop of Worcestershire sauce | Season to taste with salt, pepper and Worcestershire sauce. |

---

 This is the dressing to accompany Caesar Salad (see next page), but it is also good served with salads of sturdier leaves such as spinach.

# ANTON'S CAESAR SALAD

**SERVES 4**

| | |
|---|---|
| **2 heads Cos lettuce** | Remove and discard the outer green leaves and separate the well-shaped firm leaves from the heart of the lettuce. Wash and dry thoroughly, and keep in a cool place until needed. |
| **30 ml (2 tablespoons) olive oil**<br>**25 g (1 oz) butter**<br>**1 small garlic clove, peeled and crushed** | Heat together in a frying pan to soften the garlic. |
| **2 slices of bread, cut into 5 mm (¼ in) cubes** | Add, and fry over moderate heat until crisp and golden brown. Drain on kitchen paper and place back in a clean pan. |
| **60 g (2¼ oz) Parmesan cheese, freshly grated** | Toss in 20 g (¾ oz) of the cheese whilst the croûtons are still hot. Heat if necessary to melt the cheese. Arrange three to four lettuce leaves on individual plates. |
| **200 ml (7 fl oz) Caesar Dressing (see previous recipe)** | Drizzle some over the lettuce, along with a sprinkle of the remaining Parmesan cheese.<br>Repeat this lettuce, dressing and cheese procedure twice more, making three layers on the plates. |
| **finely cut chives** | Garnish the top layers with chives and the warm cheesy croûtons. |

*Anton's Caesar salad*

# CHEESE

Cheese – basically, solidified milk – has been enjoyed as food for thousands of years, and there must also be well over a thousand varieties. For me, to eat and cook with cheese can be an endless adventure.

The milk used to make cheese is not necessarily just that of the cow. Sheep's milk cheeses are well known and include the French Roquefort, the Italian Pecorino and Fontina, and the Greek Feta (although some are now made with cow's milk). The Italian Mozzarella was once only made with the milk of the water buffalo; cow's milk is now most normally used. Goats have been used to provide milk and cheese for many centuries, particularly in peasant cultures: the animals can exist on virtually nothing, in the most barren of terrains, therefore are more practical dairying animals than cattle or sheep. There are literally hundreds of goat cheeses, most produced on individual farms, throughout France particularly. Many excellent British goat cheeses are now being made.

In a nutritional sense, cheese is important to those who do not eat meat. It retains most of the valuable constituents of milk, providing protein, calcium and Vitamins A and D. However, it also contains a considerable proportion of fat, and many on slimming diets transfer their cheese affection to such as cottage cheese, (skimmed milk curd), *fromage frais*, Ricotta and quark. Goat's cheeses are considerably lower in calories than many other cheeses; they are also easier to digest as the milk fat particles are smaller than in cow's milk.

Many cheeses cook well – in both savoury and sweet dishes – and some cheese dishes are famous the world over; in particular the fondue of my native Switzerland. There are a number of cheese dishes elsewhere in this book, as cheese, being so versatile, goes so well with so many other foods, in breads and savoury baking, on vegetables and pasta, and in sauces. If there is difficulty in obtaining the cheese specified in a particular recipe, look for one that will perform in a similar way: for instance use a Gruyère or

*Small Glamorgan and cherry tomato grills, with
Mushroom Kebabs (see page 82)*

Emmenthal instead of an Appenzell; a Sbrinz or Pecorino instead
of fresh Parmesan; and cream or cottage cheese to replace Ricotta
or Mascarpone in pasta stuffings and sweet dishes. Get to know
those who run your local cheese shop, and never be afraid to ask
questions. I was brought up with cheese in Switzerland – there are
many wonderful varieties there – but I can still learn from the
experts.

Most cheeses should be eaten as they are for full appreciation of
texture and flavour. In Europe it is traditional to serve cheese as
a separate course, and I think this is better after the main course
and before the dessert so that it can bridge the gap between
savoury and sweet. Buy cheese carefully, store carefully, and always
allow to come to room temperature before serving; an hour out of
the refrigerator should be sufficient.

# GLAMORGAN AND CHERRY TOMATO GRILL

### MAKES 8 BROCHETTES

| | |
|---|---|
| **15 ml (1 tablespoon) vegetable oil**<br>**1 small garlic clove, peeled and chopped**<br>**1 leek, washed and finely chopped** | Sweat together gently, then cook for a couple of minutes until soft. |
| **150 g (5 oz) Caerphilly (or Cheddar) cheese, grated**<br>**30 ml (2 tablespoons) chopped parsley**<br>**2.5 ml (½ teaspoon) dry mustard powder**<br>**150 g (5 oz) fresh white breadcrumbs** | Mix together with the leek mixture. |
| **1 egg, beaten** | Stir in, to bind the mixture well together. |
| **salt and freshly ground pepper** | Taste, then season with salt and pepper. Leave to chill in the refrigerator for 30 minutes. |
| **24 red cherry tomatoes**<br>**16 yellow cherry tomatoes** | Shape the cheese mixture into walnut-sized balls (you'll need at least 32). Thread these 'Glamorgan balls' on to skewers alternately with the cherry tomatoes (3 each of the red and 2 each of the yellow). |
| **45 ml (3 tablespoons) vegetable oil** | Heat over a high heat in a large heavy frying pan. Add the skewers and cook, turning them gently with a slotted spoon, and regulating the heat so that they brown quickly and evenly without burning or breaking apart. |

 Serve as a lunch dish, on a buffet, or make smaller for canapés.

# Spinach and Cheese-Stuffed Mushrooms

**MAKES 8**

**OVEN: Moderately hot, 190°C/375°F/Gas 5**

| | |
|---|---|
| 15 ml (1 tablespoon) olive oil<br>1 shallot, peeled and finely chopped<br>1 garlic clove, peeled and finely chopped | Sweat together until soft. |
| 15 ml (1 tablespoon) finely chopped parsley<br>200 g (7 oz) spinach, washed, tough stalks removed, blanched and finely chopped | Add, and cook for another couple of minutes. Leave the mixture to cool. |
| 75 g (3 oz) Lymeswold cheese, crumbled<br>40 g (1½ oz) mature Cheddar cheese, grated<br>40 g (1½ oz) fresh white breadcrumbs<br>1 egg<br>salt and freshly ground pepper<br>freshly grated nutmeg | Add, and season to taste with salt, pepper and nutmeg. |
| 8 large field mushrooms, stems removed | Fill with the stuffing, and place in a buttered baking dish. |
| 15 ml (1 tablespoon) lemon juice<br>50 g (2 oz) butter, melted | Sprinkle over the mushrooms, and bake in the preheated oven until heated through, about 20–25 minutes. |

 Vary the flavours by varying the cheeses: Feta and Parmesan could be a good combination.

# FONDUE

| | |
|---|---|
| **1 garlic clove, peeled and halved** | Rub over the inside of an earthenware fondue pot, or caclon or *caquelon* as it is known in Switzerland. Place on the stove. |
| **400 ml (14 fl oz) dry white wine** | Pour in and bring almost to the boil. |
| **400 g (14 oz) each of Gruyère and Emmenthal cheeses** | Grate, and add, and stir continuously with a wooden spoon until the cheese has melted and the mixture reaches boiling point. |
| **approx. 15 ml (1 tablespoon) cornflour, diluted in 15 ml (1 tablespoon) Kirsch**<br>**salt and freshly ground pepper**<br>**freshly grated nutmeg**<br>**a pinch of cayenne** | Add, and season to taste with salt, pepper, nutmeg and cayenne.<br>Transfer the pot to a spirit burner over a low flame on the table. |
| **700 g – 1 kg (1½– 2¼ lb) bread with crust, or Zopf (see page 32)** | Cut into 2.5 cm (1 in) squares, and place in a bowl. Skewer these with fondue forks, and dip into the fondue. |

Stir the fondue often, enabling it to combine and not separate. Beside the traditional bread cubes served with fondue, there are a few more possibilities: try breadsticks, herb or onion breads, assorted cooked vegetables, new potatoes and even cooked pasta shells and tortellini.

There are numerous variations on fondue; in Switzerland, they vary from canton to canton. Vary the cheeses too if you like, but Gruyère and Emmenthal are *the* cheeses for fondue.

# CHEESE SOUFFLÉ

**SERVES 4**

**OVEN:** Moderately hot, 180°C/350°F/Gas 4

| | |
|---|---|
| 10 g (¼ oz) butter<br>finely grated cheese for<br>  coating | Butter and coat the inside of a large soufflé dish with cheese. Turn and shake off any surplus. |
| 50 g (2 oz) butter<br>25 g (1 oz) plain flour | Melt the butter in a pan and add the flour. Stir to a paste, then cook for about 3 minutes. |
| 250 ml (8 fl oz) milk | Gradually add, whisking continuously, until it is a thick mixture resembling béchamel. Remove from the heat. |
| 4 eggs, separated<br>150 g (5 oz) Cheddar<br>  cheese, grated<br>salt, cayenne and<br>  nutmeg<br>5 ml (1 teaspoon)<br>  cornflour | Add the egg yolks and cheese and season with salt, cayenne and nutmeg.<br>Whisk the egg whites with a pinch of salt and the cornflour until stiff. Take a third of the egg white and mix into the cheese mixture.<br>Fold in the remainder using a spatula. Fill the prepared soufflé dish.<br>Bake for 20–25 minutes until risen and golden. Serve immediately. |

 The mixture can be baked in small cocottes in which case they will take about 7–8 minutes to cook.
Garnish the top with triangles of thinly sliced cheese if you like.

# Goat Cheese Marinated in Peppercorns and Thyme

**SERVES 4**

| | |
|---|---|
| **1 × 350 g (12 oz) log of mild goat cheese, cut crosswise into 4**<br>**22.5 ml (1½ tablespoons) mixed peppercorns, crushed**<br>**6–8 sprigs of thyme** | Place in a 500 ml (18 fl oz) jar with a tight-fitting lid. |
| **400–500 ml (14–18 fl oz) olive oil** | Pour in enough to cover the cheese completely.<br>Cover and chill for 1–4 weeks, to allow the cheese to marinate.<br>Let the cheese come to room temperature before serving. |

*M* Instead of the peppercorns and thyme, you could add crushed fennel seeds, dried red chilli peppers, rosemary sprigs, lemon zest or garlic.
You could also marinate individual small cheeses. We used for the picture several *petits crottins*, scraped off the skin, and marinated them in the oil with the peppercorns, adding a few sprigs of rosemary, a few pieces of sun-dried tomato, some garlic and flat parsley.

*Goat cheese marinated in peppercorns and thyme*

# CHEESE SNACKS OR CANAPÉS

### BRIE OR CAMEMBERT
Cut into 1 cm (½ in) cubes. Dip in beaten egg, coat with fine fresh breadcrumbs, and toss in a hot pan with a little fat (or deep-fry). Drain on absorbent paper and eat in the fingers or sprinkle over salads.

### MINI GOLF BALLS
Form your favourite soft or goat cheese into walnut-sized balls, then roll either in freshly cut chives, paprika, chopped roasted nuts, poppy or sesame seeds, or chopped sweet peppers.

### CHEESY GRAPE SURPRISES
Take a ½ teaspoonful of cream cheese in the palm of one hand and roll it around a grape, coating evenly. Roll the cheese-wrapped grapes in chopped roasted almonds, walnuts, pine kernels or pistachio nuts. (Prepare cherries in the same way.)

# CROÛTE AU FROMAGE

**SERVES 4**

| | |
|---|---|
| 1 shallot, peeled and finely chopped<br>40 g (1½ oz) butter | Sweat together for a few minutes. |
| 300 g (11 oz) wild mushrooms in season (chanterelles, ceps)<br>salt and freshly ground pepper | Add, and cook over high heat for approximately 4 minutes. Season with salt and pepper. |
| 30 ml (2 tablespoons) white wine<br>60 ml (4 tablespoons) single cream<br>5 ml (1 teaspoon) freshly cut marjoram | Add, and bring quickly to the boil. Cook until the liquid has almost evaporated. Adjust the seasoning. |

| | |
|---|---|
| **4 slices bread** | Toast on both sides, then divide the mushroom mixture evenly between the slices. |
| **200 g (7 oz) Emmenthal or Gruyère cheese, sliced** | Place over the mushroom toasts, and brown under the hot grill. |
| **parsley leaves** | Serve immediately, garnished with parsley leaves. |

**M** Sautéed spinach could be served this way, by itself, or mixed with some mushrooms. Add a dash of cream to the spinach. Serve as a snack or a lunch dish, or cut up into small squares to serve with drinks as canapés.

# GOAT CHEESE AND TOMATO TOAST

**MAKES 32–36**

**OVEN:** Moderately hot, 190°C/375°F/Gas 5

| | |
|---|---|
| **1 *baguette*, cut diagonally into slices** **garlic oil (see page 137)** | Drizzle one side of the *baguette* slices with garlic oil and toast both sides. |
| **225 g (8 oz) herbed goat's cheese** | Cream and spread over the oiled side of each slice. |
| **8 pieces of sun-dried tomato in oil, roughly chopped** | Scatter on top of the cheese. Place the slices on a baking tray and bake in the preheated oven for 2–3 minutes until the cheese starts to sizzle. (Or simply grill.) |
| **basil leaves** | Sprinkle over the toasts, and serve warm. |

# Blue Cheese Dressing

**MAKES ABOUT 120 ML (4 FL OZ)**

75 g (3 oz) Roquefort or
Stilton cheese,
crumbled
60 ml (4 tablespoons)
olive oil
100 g (4 oz) natural
yoghurt
30 ml (2 tablespoons)
sherry vinegar
salt and pepper

Combine all the ingredients in a liquidiser and mix
until fairly smooth.
Season to taste with salt and pepper.

---

This is particularly good as a dressing for 'tougher' lettuce
leaves such as Cos and Webb's lettuce, and spinach.
It is also very good with thin raw slices of kohlrabi (see page
150). Leave out the yoghurt if you want a less 'creamy'
dressing, or *fromage frais* can be used *instead* of yoghurt.

# Walnut Goat Cheese Sauce

**MAKES ABOUT 200 ML (7 FL OZ)**

50 g (2 oz) shelled
walnuts
a little milk

Blanch the walnuts in milk, and then peel off the
brown skin. Chop coarsely.

---

15 ml (1 tablespoon)
walnut oil

Heat and fry the chopped walnuts for a few minutes.

---

100 g (4 oz) goat cheese
(*chabis*), crumbled
100 ml (3½ fl oz)
*fromage frais*
30 ml (2 tablespoons)
vegetable stock (see
page 24)

Add, and stir until thoroughly mixed and cheese has
melted. You may need a little extra stock to thin to
the required consistency.

---

| | |
|---|---|
| 15 ml (1 tablespoon)<br>  finely cut chives<br>salt and freshly ground<br>  pepper<br>cayenne pepper<br>lemon juice to taste | Add, and correct seasoning with salt, pepper,<br>cayenne and lemon juice. |

This sauce is delicious with the Broccoli Mousses on page 80. It also goes well with pasta.
It will keep in the refrigerator for a few days.

# BLUE CHEESE SAUCE

## MAKES ABOUT 500 ML (18 FL OZ)

| | |
|---|---|
| 500 ml (18 fl oz) milk | Warm through in a large pan. |
| 50 g (2 oz) butter | Melt in a thick-bottomed pan. |
| 50 g (2 oz) plain flour | Add to the butter and mix in well. Cook for a few minutes over a gentle heat without colouring. Gradually add the warmed milk and stir until smooth. Allow to simmer for approximately 10 minutes. |
| 50 g (2 oz) blue cheese,<br>  grated | Add, then remove from the heat. |
| 1 egg yolk<br>salt and cayenne<br>  pepper | Mix in well, then strain the sauce and season to taste with salt and cayenne. |
| 30 ml (2 tablespoons)<br>  whipping cream,<br>  whipped | Fold in, and serve. |

Serve with pasta – it's delicious with gnocchi (see page 128).
Stilton would be good, Roquefort or Gorgonzola.

# Lemon Cheese Snow with Apricot Coulis

**SERVES 4–6**

**2 leaves of gelatine, soaked, or 10 ml (2 teaspoons) powdered gelatine**
**juice of 1 lemon**

Dissolve the gelatine in the lemon juice.

---

**500 g (18 oz) Ricotta cheese**
**finely grated rind of 1 lemon**

Whisk together. Add a little of this to the gelatine, and return to the bulk of the cheese.

---

**3 egg whites**
**60 g (2½ oz) caster sugar**

Beat together until stiff, then fold into the cheese. Spoon into one large dish or six individual ramekins and chill for at least 1 hour.

---

**300 g (11 oz) ripe apricots, stoned**
**90 ml (6 tablespoons) icing sugar, or to taste**

For the sauce, purée together in a liquidiser (reserving six neat quarters of apricot for decoration). Strain into a jug.

---

**6 sprigs of mint**

Serve either straight from the ramekin decorated with the reserved apricot pieces and mint leaves, with the sauce handed separately, or spoon out on to plates with the sauce and decorate.

---

The Ricotta 'snow' may be served with the apricot *coulis* as a pudding, or it can be used as a soft creamy accompaniment for a compote (see page 197).
Other fruit *coulis* may be made in the same way – raspberry or strawberry, for instance.

*Lemon cheese snow with Apricot compote (see page 197)*

# CURD CHEESE SOUFFLÉ WITH PASSION-FRUIT SAUCE

**SERVES 4**

**OVEN:** Moderate, 180°C/350°F/Gas 4

| | |
|---|---|
| **500 g (18 oz) *fromage blanc*** <br> **120 ml (4 fl oz) skimmed milk** <br> **3 eggs, separated** | Beat together the *fromage blanc*, milk and egg yolks. Whisk the egg whites until almost stiff. |
| **30 g (1¼ oz) cornflour** <br> **30 g (1¼ oz) icing sugar, or to taste** | Add to the egg whites and whisk until stiff. Fold the egg whites into the *fromage blanc* mixture. Butter and sugar a non-stick soufflé dish approximately 15 cm (6 in) in diameter. Fill with the soufflé mixture. Bake in the preheated oven for about 25 minutes, until risen and golden. |
| **30 g (1¼ oz) caster sugar** <br> **100 ml (3½ fl oz) water** | Meanwhile, for the sauce, bring to the boil together to dissolve the sugar. |
| **6 passion fruit, halved** | Spoon the pulp of the passion fruit into the blender, and whizz briefly to separate the seeds from the golden juice. Strain into the syrup and bring to the boil. |
| **5 ml (1 teaspoon) cornflour diluted in 45 ml (3 tablespoons) water** | Whisk into the sauce, and continue to boil until it lightly coats a spoon. Serve the soufflé as soon as it is ready, in spoonfuls on a pool of the sauce. |

A hot soufflé is an ideal pudding for the autumn and winter – and makes a much lighter finish to the meal than the traditional boiled or baked puddings.
The sauce is also very good served with a chocolate bombe (see page 216).

# Peaches with Goat Cheese and Gingernut Biscuits

**SERVES 4**

**OVEN:** Moderately hot, 200°C/400°F/Gas 6

| | |
|---|---|
| **4 ripe peaches** | Blanch and skin, then cut in halves, twist to open and remove the stones. |
| **200 ml (7 fl oz) sugar syrup (see below)** | Heat in a pan large enough to hold the peach halves, and poach them for 2–3 minutes. Drain and cool. |
| **175 g (6 oz) very fresh goat cheese (*chabis*)** | Mix, crush and divide into eight equal pieces. Roll each piece into a ball. |
| **4 gingernut biscuits, crushed into fine crumbs** | Spread on a plate, and roll each cheese ball in it until well coated. Place a cheese ball into each hollow of the peach halves, then arrange the halves in a baking dish. Bake in the preheated oven for approximately 5 minutes until the crumbs become crisp and the peaches are warm. |
| **250 ml (8 fl oz) raspberry coulis (see page 166)** **4 sprigs of mint** | Serve the peach halves on a bed of raspberry *coulis*, decorated with sprigs of mint. |

Drained *fromage blanc* is a good substitute if very fresh goat cheese is not available.

To make sugar syrup, bring 1 litre (1¾ pints) water and 500 g (18 oz) granulated sugar to the boil together. Simmer until the sugar has dissolved, about 2 minutes. Use as required.

# CHEESECAKE

Grease a 23–23 cm (8–9 in) loose-bottomed cake tin with extra butter.

| | |
|---|---|
| **50 g (2 oz) unsalted butter** | Melt slowly in a pan. |
| **175 g (6 oz) digestive or gingernut biscuits, made into crumbs** | Mix into the butter, and then press this mixture into an even layer all over the base of the cake tin. Leave to set. |
| **350 g (12 oz) soft cream cheese**<br>**90 g (3½ oz) caster sugar**<br>**finely grated rind of 1 lemon** | Beat together until soft and creamy. |
| **2 egg yolks** | Beat in, one at a time, until light and fluffy. |
| **300 ml (10 fl oz) double cream**<br>**10 ml (2 teaspoons) Kirsch** | Beat together until the cream just holds soft peaks. |
| **2 egg whites** | Whisk until stiff. |
| **juice of 1 lemon**<br>**4 gelatine leaves, soaked in cold water to soften** | Heat the lemon juice, add the soaked gelatine, and dissolve.<br>Stir the gelatine into the cheese mixture and beat well together.<br>Fold in the whipped cream and beaten egg white.<br>Pour the mixture into the prepared biscuit-lined tin, and chill until set, about 1–2 hours. |

*An individual cheesecake*

**45 ml (3 tablespoons) water**
**30 ml (2 tablespoons) fresh lemon juice**
**25 g (1 oz) caster sugar**

For the topping, heat together until the sugar dissolves.

---

**1 gelatine leaf, soaked in cold water to soften**

Add, and leave to cool but not set. Gently spoon this liquid over the cheesecake, and leave to set.

---

Different flavourings as well as different toppings can be added. For an orange rather than lemon cheesecake, add finely grated orange rind and orange juice to the cheese mixture, and decorate the top with orange segments or slices. Berries could be used on the top as well.

You can make small individual cheesecakes in individual moulds. In the photograph overleaf we decorated the basic cheesecake with fine slices of blood orange with their skins, which had been cooked in the topping.

Serve the cheesecakes, large or small, with a fruit *coulis* (see page 166).

# MASCARPONE AND RASPBERRY CRÈME BRÛLÉE

### SERVES 8

| | |
|---|---|
| **225 g (8 oz) raspberries** | Divide between eight 150 ml (5 fl oz) ramekins. |
| **8 egg yolks**<br>**50 g (2 oz) caster sugar**<br>**100 g (4 oz)**<br>  **Mascarpone cheese** | Whisk together. |
| **500 ml (18 fl oz)**<br>  **whipping cream**<br>**1 vanilla pod, split** | Bring to the boil together, then pour into the egg yolk mixture and blend well.<br>Return the mixture to the pan, then place on the stove, stirring constantly over very gentle heat until it thickens, taking care not to let the mixture boil and curdle.<br>Strain the mixture into the ramekins, cool and chill for at least 4 hours or overnight. |
| **demerara sugar** | Sprinkle evenly over the top of the ramekins. Place under a hot grill, to melt and caramelise the sugar. Chill the ramekins again for an hour or so before serving. |

You can also make the crème brûlée with pitted cherries, stoned and sliced peaches and apricots.

Mascarpone, an Italian cow's milk cream cheese, is the main ingredient in the famous Tiramisù, a dessert which is a speciality of the Veneto.

# AFTERNOON TEA AND SWEET BAKING

Afternoon tea is a quintessentially English ritual, but similar mid-afternoon feasts occur all over Europe. I was in Budapest recently, at the Gerbéaud *Pâtisserie*, and there they take the afternoon cakes and coffee (rather than tea) very seriously indeed. You must go to one of the well-known hotels in London to enjoy the supreme British afternoon tea, but famous places in Lausanne, Zurich, Vienna, Berlin, Munich, Florence and Venice (and many others), also serve afternoon coffee and tea accompanied by cakes, *strudels*, frangipane tarts and *pâtisserie* of all kinds.

The English afternoon tea is reputed to have come into being because of the between breakfast and dinner hunger of an eighteenth-century Duchess of Bedford. She covertly ordered slivers of bread and butter, small cakes and pots of tea, a secret feast which soon became known to other ladies of her acquaintance and became a popular institution.

The ritual gradually became more elaborate, with savouries such as sausage rolls, thin elegant sandwiches with cucumber or potted meat fillings, and buttered toast or muffins. This expansion of the content of a tea brought the new fashion nearer to the older British, more rural, tradition of *high* tea, a meal that often replaced dinner and included a few small hot cooked dishes, savoury pasties, cold meat, preserves and bread and butter.

I am glad that afternoon tea is enjoying a revival in Britain, as it is one of my favourite meals of the day. My home country of Switzerland is renowned for its *pâtisserie*, and there are several ideas reproduced here. The *vacherin* with yoghurt ice may seem to be an unlikely offering, but it would be wonderful at a special celebration tea. *Strudels* are very Central European, but ideal fare to accompany a pot of tea or coffee; and they needn't of course be sweet

*Mosimann's muesli pancakes, some half-way through cooking*

(see page 46). I like the idea of serving savoury foods at tea time, and I'm also very keen on the idea of offering *small* items; you can have quite a few tastes, not just one large eclair which spoils your appetite for anything else!

I have included a number of European-inspired preserves to spread on the breads, muffins and scones of afternoon tea. These are much fruitier, less set than those bought or made at home in Britain. They contain less sugar and therefore are considerably less sweet. And do not forget that many of the bread and savoury baking recipes in Chapter Two and most of the chocolate recipes in the next chapter, would quite naturally take their place in an afternoon tea spread.

# MOSIMANN'S
# MUESLI PANCAKES

**MAKES ABOUT 24**

60 g (2¼ oz) medium
  oatflakes
1 large egg, beaten
150 ml (5 fl oz) milk
a pinch of salt
10 ml (2 teaspoons)
  baking powder
6 pieces dried apricot
2 pieces dried pear
30 ml (2 tablespoons)
  raisins
15 ml (1 tablespoon)
  chopped nuts
1 apple, grated

Mix all the ingredients together and let the mixture rest for approximately 30–60 minutes for the oatflakes to swell.

butter for greasing

Heat a frying pan or griddle and grease with a little butter. Drop the batter in by the dessertspoonful, about three at a time. Cook slowly until the edge starts to set, approximately 3 minutes, then turn over and cook the other side until lightly browned. Keep warm.
Repeat until the mixture is finished.

icing sugar

Serve immediately with a dusting of icing sugar.

Honey or compote and some Greek yoghurt will go well with these drop scones.
They are good for breakfast, afternoon tea or dessert.

# DROP SCONES

**MAKES ABOUT 18**

100 g (4 oz) self-raising
  flour
30 g (1¼ oz) caster
  sugar

Mix together in a bowl and make a well in the centre.

| 1 egg, beaten<br>120–150 ml (4–5 fl oz)<br>  milk | Stir in, and mix to the consistency of thick cream. Drop the mixture in tablespoons on to a greased hot griddle or heavy-based frying pan, three at a time. Cook until they start to bubble, then turn over and cook for another minute until golden brown. |

Keep the scones warm by wrapping them in a clean teatowel. Served warm with butter or honey, they're good for breakfast or afternoon tea, as are the muffins below.

# BANANA AND PECAN MUFFINS

**MAKES ABOUT 12**

**OVEN: Moderate, 180°C/350°F/Gas 4**

| 100 g (4 oz) unsalted<br>  butter<br>100 g (4 oz) caster<br>  sugar | Cream together until light in a large bowl. |
| 2 eggs, beaten | Add, and mix together well. |
| 200 g (7 oz) plain flour<br>10 ml (2 teaspoons)<br>  baking powder<br>a pinch of salt<br>2.5 ml (½ teaspoon)<br>  each of powdered<br>  cinnamon and<br>  ground ginger<br>a pinch of ground<br>  cloves | Sift together and add to the bowl. |
| 100 ml (3½ fl oz) milk<br>50 g (2 oz) raisins<br>100 g (4 oz) pecan nuts,<br>  roughly chopped<br>4 ripe bananas, peeled<br>  and mashed | Add to the bowl, and mix well together.<br>Pour the batter into greased muffin tins, and bake in the preheated oven for 15 minutes. |

# APPLE AND CARROT RAISIN MUFFINS

**MAKES ABOUT 18**

**OVEN:** Moderately hot, 200°C/400°F/Gas 6

| | |
|---|---|
| 250 g (9 oz) plain flour<br>15 ml (1 tablespoon)<br>  baking powder<br>5 ml (1 teaspoon)<br>  powdered cinnamon<br>a pinch of salt<br>100 g (4 oz) soft brown<br>  sugar | Sieve together into a mixing bowl. |
| 1 eating apple, peeled,<br>  cored and grated<br>100 g (4 oz) carrot,<br>  finely grated<br>50 g (2 oz) shredded<br>  coconut<br>50 g (2 oz) raisins<br>50 g (2 oz) pumpkin<br>  seeds, lightly toasted<br>30 ml (2 tablespoons)<br>  bran cereal (All-Bran) | Add, and mix together. |
| 2 eggs, beaten<br>100 g (4 oz) unsalted<br>  butter, melted<br>30 ml (2 tablespoons)<br>  milk<br>a few drops of vanilla<br>  essence | Mix together, and stir into the dry ingredients. Blend well.<br>Spoon the mixture into greased muffin tins and bake in the preheated oven for approximately 20 minutes until firm to the touch and lightly browned. Let the muffins rest in the tin for a couple of minutes before turning out. |
| icing sugar | Dust with icing sugar. |

Serve warm for breakfast or afternoon tea.

# ENGLISH MUFFINS

**MAKES ABOUT 18**

**OVEN:** Very hot, 240°C/475°F/Gas 9

| | |
|---|---|
| 15 g (½ oz) fresh yeast<br>250 ml (8 fl oz) hand-<br>  hot milk<br>5 ml (1 teaspoon) caster<br>  sugar | Blend together. |
| 1 egg<br>30 g (1¼ oz) unsalted<br>  butter, melted | Lightly beat together. |
| 450 g (1 lb) plain flour<br>a pinch of salt | Sift together into a mixing bowl and make a well in the centre.<br>Pour in the yeast mixture and the egg and butter mixture. Mix to a dough.<br>Turn out on to a clean working surface and knead until smooth and elastic. Place the dough back in the bowl, cover and leave in a warm place until doubled in size (approximately 40 minutes).<br>Turn out the risen dough and knead lightly. Roll out to about 1 cm (½ in) thick. Using a floured cutter, cut into 6 cm (2½ in) rounds. Knead the trimmings together and roll and cut them out in the same way. Place the muffins on a lightly greased and heated griddle or frying pan. Cook gently over low heat for about 6 minutes on each side until golden brown. Alternatively bake in the preheated oven for 5 minutes until they are slightly browned, then turn them over and finish cooking (about another 10–15 minutes). |

 I like to make small bite-sized muffins, substituting half the plain flour with rye or wholemeal flour, or adding some spinach or tomato purée, plus herbs and spices, as a base for canapés.

# APPLE AND FRANGIPANE TART

**MAKES A 20 CM (8 IN) TART**

**OVEN: Moderately hot, 190°C/375°F/Gas 5**

150 g (5 oz) plain flour, sifted

For the sweet pastry, place in a mound on a clean work surface, and make a well in the centre.

100 g (4 oz) unsalted butter, cut into cubes
30 g (1¼ oz) icing sugar, sifted
1 egg yolk
finely grated rind of ½ lemon

Add to the well, and work together, gradually incorporating the flour, to a smooth paste.
Roll into a ball and rest for at least 20–30 minutes in the refrigerator.
Roll out and use to line the greased tart tin. Leave in a cool place for about 20–30 minutes.

25 g (1 oz) unsalted butter
75 g (3 oz) brown sugar

For the filling, heat the butter and sugar together in a heavy-bottomed frying pan until the sugar dissolves.

4 cooking apples, peeled and cored
30 g (1¼ oz) currants

Cut each apple into eight wedges. Add apples and currants to the pan, and sauté quickly for approximately 5 minutes.

30 ml (2 tablespoons) Amaretto liqueur

Flame with the Amaretto, then remove pan from the heat and leave to cool.

100 g (4 oz) unsalted butter
100 g (4 oz) caster sugar

For the frangipane, cream together until light and creamy.

1 large egg, beaten
100 g (4 oz) ground almonds
30 g (1¼ oz) plain flour
15 ml (1 tablespoon) milk

Fold in.
Spread the frangipane over the tart base, and smooth the top. Arrange the apple slices around the top of the cake. Spoon the currants and any juices over.
Bake in the preheated oven for approximately 30–35

*A selection of afternoon tea delights including Chocolate brownies (see page 204) and small Apple and frangipane (and fruit) tarts*

minutes until cooked and lightly golden brown in colour.
Remove from the oven and transfer to a wire rack.

| | |
|---|---|
| **100 g (4 oz) apricot glaze (see below)** | While the tart is still warm brush the top with the hot apricot glaze. |

Serve with an ice cream for dessert, or an afternoon tea treat. You could make small individual frangipane (or fruit) tarts. For apricot glaze, simply melt apricot jam over a gentle heat, sieve and brush on food as appropriate.

# MARZIPAN AND CRANBERRY CAKE

### MAKES A 20 CM (8 IN) CAKE

**OVEN:** Moderately hot, 180°C/350°F/Gas 4

Butter a 20 cm (8 in) round cake tin with extra butter.

| | |
|---|---|
| **200 g (7 oz) almond paste or marzipan**<br>**75 g (3 oz) unsalted butter**<br>**50 g (2 oz) caster sugar** | Cream together until smooth. |
| **3 eggs, beaten** | Add, then beat in well. |
| **150 g (5 oz) cranberries, chopped**<br>**100 g (4 oz) ground almonds**<br>**100 g (4 oz) plain flour**<br>**10 ml (2 teaspoons) baking powder** | Fold in.<br>Pour the mixture into the greased tin and bake in the preheated oven for approximately 40 minutes.<br>Turn out on to a cooling tray. |
| **100 g (4 oz) marmalade**<br>**30 ml (2 tablespoons) water** | Heat together and cook to a glaze. Brush over the cake, then leave to become completely cold. |

# Wholewheat Gingerbread

**FILLS A 15 × 23 CM (6 × 9 IN) TIN**

**OVEN:** Moderate, 180°C/350°F/Gas 4

Line the cake tin with good greaseproof paper, then grease with extra butter.

| | |
|---|---|
| 120 g (4½ oz) plain flour<br>a pinch of salt<br>5 ml (1 level teaspoon) mixed spice<br>15 ml (3 level teaspoons) ground ginger | Sift into a bowl. |
| 120 g (4½ oz) wholemeal flour<br>40 g (1½ oz) demerara sugar<br>40 g (1½ oz) each of sultanas and chopped mixed peel | Stir in. |
| 120 g (4½ oz) each of unsalted butter, golden syrup and black treacle | Place together in a saucepan and heat gently until melted. Add to the dry ingredients and mix. |
| 5 ml (1 level teaspoon) bicarbonate of soda<br>120 ml (4½ fl oz) warm milk<br>1 egg, beaten | Dissolve the bicarbonate of soda in the warm milk and add the beaten egg. Pour into the mixture and beat to form a smooth batter. Pour into the tin. |
| 25 g (1 oz) flaked almonds | Scatter over the top of the batter, then bake in the centre of the preheated oven for 40–45 minutes until well risen and springy to the touch.<br>Cool slightly in the tin before turning out on to a cooling tray. Remove the paper, and leave to cool. Store in an airtight tin for 2–3 days before cutting. |

# BRIOCHE

## MAKES 1 LOAF OR ABOUT 20 ROLLS

**OVEN: Moderately hot, 200°C/400°F/Gas 6**

| | |
|---|---|
| **15 g (½ oz) fresh yeast**<br>**5 ml (1 teaspoon) honey**<br>**100 ml (3½ fl oz)**<br>**lukewarm water** | Cream the yeast with the honey, then add the lukewarm water. Mix well. |
| **500 g (18 oz) strong**<br>**plain flour** | Add 100 g (4 oz) of the flour, and mix into a thin batter. Cover and set aside in a warm place for about 30 minutes. Place the remaining flour in a bowl and make a well in the centre. |
| **150 g (5 oz) soft butter** | Cream until soft. |
| **5 ml (1 teaspoon) salt**<br>**4 eggs, beaten** | Add to the well in the flour along with the creamed butter and the yeast mixture. Mix to form a dough. Knead on an unfloured surface for about 5 minutes until smooth, elastic and shiny.<br>Chill for 30–40 minutes.<br>If making rolls, divide the dough into 50 g (2 oz) pieces. Divide each piece into two-thirds and one-third. Roll the bigger pieces into balls and place in 20 greased small brioche moulds. Using a wooden spoon handle, make an indentation in each roll and brush inside with water. Put the smaller pieces, also rolled into balls, into the holes. Cover and allow to rise in a warm place for about 30–40 minutes. |
| **1 egg, beaten** | Brush over the risen rolls, and bake in the preheated oven for about 15 minutes until golden brown. Cool. If making one large loaf, use a 1 litre (1¾ pint) brioche mould, also buttered. Cut about one-sixth off the dough to make the 'hat', and egg wash and bake in the oven for 45–50 minutes, covering with foil if it is browning too quickly. |

Brioche can be baked in ordinary tins if you haven't got the special moulds.
You could brush the top of the brioche with a glaze of marmalade to get a shiny and sweet-tasting topping.

# Strudel Pastry

**SERVES 10–12**

**OVEN:** Moderately hot, 200°C/400°F/Gas 6

**250 g (9 oz) strong plain flour**
**5 g (⅛ oz) salt**

Preheat a large metal bowl in the oven.
Sift flour and salt on to the work surface, and make a well in the centre.

**1 egg, beaten**
**25 ml (1 fl oz) sunflower oil**
**175 ml (6 fl oz) warm water**

Add to the well in the flour, then, using your fingertips, gradually mix the flour in from the sides, drawing more in as the dough thickens.
Knead until smooth, about 7–10 minutes, then form into a ball. Place on a lightly floured board, brush with some extra oil, and invert the heated bowl over to cover. Leave for about 30–60 minutes to rest.
Cover a large work surface – a table is best – with a clean sheet or tablecloth. Lightly flour it and roll the dough to as large and thin a square as possible.
Flour your hands, place them under the dough, and raise the dough. Starting at the centre and working outwards, carefully stretch the dough with both hands. Continue to work outwards as the dough gets thinner. It should be so transparent that you can read a newspaper through it! The ideal size is about 1 metre (40 in) square. Trim off the thick edges.

**65 g (2½ oz) butter, melted**

Brush all over the pastry, using half only, then spoon on your chosen filling at one end of the pastry, leaving a good 15 cm (6 in) border all round. Flip the border over the filling all round, then with the aid of the cloth, start rolling the strudel up.
Transfer the roll to a greased baking sheet. Bend and shape it into a crescent if necessary.
Brush with the remaining melted butter and bake in the preheated oven for 30–40 minutes until brown and crisp. Baste occasionally with more butter.

Strudel pastry *is* difficult to make at home; bought filo pastry can be used instead.

Overleaf, from left: *Prune and quark, Apple and raisin, and a Potato and leek strudel with added spinach and cheese (see page 46)*

# Apple Strudel Filling

| | |
|---|---|
| **65 g (2½ oz) fine white breadcrumbs, toasted** | Sprinkle over the prepared sheet of strudel pastry. |
| **1 kg (2¼ lb) apples**<br>**lemon juice**<br>**100 g (4 oz) soft brown sugar**<br>**65 g (2½ oz) sultanas**<br>**65 g (2½ oz) chopped nuts**<br>**powdered cinnamon** | Peel, core and thinly slice the apples. Sprinkle with lemon juice (and a little white wine if you like).<br>Mix all together for the filling, and place on top of the breadcrumbs.<br>Roll as in the basic recipe. |
| **50 g (2 oz) butter, melted** | Brush over the strudel and bake as in the basic recipe, basting from time to time. |
| **icing sugar** | Sprinkle over the strudel 5 minutes before the end of cooking time to give a golden glaze. |

# Apricot and Marzipan Strudel Filling

| | |
|---|---|
| **200 g (7 oz) good marzipan**<br>**150 ml (5 fl oz) double cream** | Cream and soften together. |
| **1.25 kg (2¾ lb) apricots, stoned and chopped**<br>**50 g (2 oz) white bread dice, dried** | Fold in.<br>Place the filling on the prepared sheet of strudel pastry, and roll as in the basic recipe. |

| | |
|---|---|
| 50 g (2 oz) butter, melted | Brush over the strudel and bake as in the basic recipe, basting from time to time. |
| icing sugar | Use to glaze as above. |

# Prune, Quark and Almond Strudel Filling

| | |
|---|---|
| 2 eggs<br>120 g (4½ oz) caster sugar | Whisk together until smooth. |
| 750 g (1 lb, 10 oz) quark or Ricotta cheese | Add and blend well. |
| 500 g (18 oz) prunes, soaked and stoned<br>75 g (3 oz) ground almonds<br>40 g (1½ oz) almonds, roughly chopped | Fold in. |
| 30 ml (2 tablespoons) fresh breadcrumbs<br>powdered cinnamon | Sprinkle on to the prepared sheet of strudel dough. Place the filling on top, and roll as in the basic recipe. |
| 50 g (2 oz) butter, melted | Brush over the strudel and bake as in the basic recipe, basting from time to time. |
| icing sugar | Use to glaze as above. |

Sour cherries also go very well with quark and Ricotta.

# Vacherin with Yoghurt Fruit Ice

**SERVES 12**

| | |
|---|---|
| **2 × 20 cm (8 in) Baked Meringue discs (see page 192)** | Place a deep cake or flan ring the same diameter as the meringue discs on a cake board. Place one disc into the ring. |
| **1 quantity Yoghurt Fruit Ice (see page 192)** | Place in scoopfuls into the ring on top of the meringue, filling to the top. Smooth the top, then cover with the remaining meringue disc. Cover, then put the board plus vacherin into the freezer to harden for at least 30 minutes. Take the vacherin out of the freezer, and carefully remove the ring. |
| **120 ml (4 fl oz) whipping cream or quark, whipped** | Spread thinly over the outside edges and top of the vacherin. |
| **seasonal berries to taste** | Use to decorate the vacherin along with rosettes of the remaining cream if liked. Serve immediately, or place back in the freezer until required. |

I like to make individual-sized vacherins filled with a seasonal icecream (chestnut is good), or simply vanilla ice, served with Chocolate Sauce (see page 213).

*A miniature Vacherin with chocolate sauce decorated with yoghurt*

# Baked Meringue

**MAKES 2 × 20 CM (8 IN) DISCS**

**OVEN:** Very cool, 110°C/225°F/Gas ¼

Draw two 20 cm (8 in) circles on a sheet of greaseproof paper, and invert the piece of paper on to a baking sheet.

| | |
|---|---|
| **4 egg whites** | With a balloon whisk, beat until stiff. |
| **200 g (7 oz) caster sugar** | Sprinkle in little by little, beating constantly after each addition until all the sugar has been beaten in, and the meringue is glossy and forms stiff peaks. Place the meringue mixture into a piping bag with a 5 mm (¼ in) round plain tube. Starting in the middle, pipe in a flat spiral on to the paper, using the pencilled circles as a guide, to get two meringue discs. Bake in the slow oven for 1–2 hours. The aim is to cook the meringue without colouring until it is crisp and dry. Transfer to a rack to cool. |

 The meringue mixture can be piped into smaller sized rounds for individual vacherins, or afternoon tea meringues.

# Yoghurt Fruit Ice

| | |
|---|---|
| **750 g (1 lb, 10 oz) berries (strawberries, raspberries, blackberries etc)** **90 ml (6 tablespoons) lemon juice** | Liquidise together, and pass through a sieve. |
| **225 g (8 oz) low-fat natural yoghurt** **225 g (8 oz) caster sugar** | Whisk together, then mix with the fruit purée. |

| | |
|---|---|
| **225 g (8 oz) quark** | Beat until smooth, then carefully fold into the fruit mixture.<br>Place in a suitable container and freeze until solid. Whisk the ice vigorously from time to time to get rid of ice particles. Or simply transfer to a *sorbetière* and churn to freeze. |

# CRÊPES

### MAKES 14–15 × 18 CM (7 IN) CRÊPES

| | |
|---|---|
| **100 g (4 oz) plain flour**<br>**a pinch of salt** | Sieve together into a bowl, and make a well in the centre. |
| **2 eggs, beaten**<br>**250 ml (8 fl oz) milk** | Mix together, then add to the well and mix, gradually incorporating the flour from the sides. Whisk to a smooth batter. |
| **25 g (1 oz) butter,**<br>  **melted** | Mix in, and leave the batter to stand for approximately 30 minutes. |
| **40 g (1½ oz) butter** | Heat a pancake pan with a knob of the butter. Add enough batter – about a small ladleful – just to cover the bottom of the pan thinly. Fry the crêpe quickly over medium heat until it is set on top and brown underneath. Turn and cook the other side. Remove to a plate and cover with a cloth if wanting to serve warm.<br>Continue making the crêpes until the batter is used up. Pile the crêpes on top of each other to keep them moist. |

For herb crêpes, add chopped parsley, chives, chervil etc to the batter.
For buckwheat crêpes, use half buckwheat flour and half the chosen flour, plain or wholemeal.
For a sweet crêpe, add about 30 g (1¼ oz) caster sugar to the batter, or to taste.
The crêpes can be frozen, interleaved with greaseproof paper.

# BLUEBERRY JAM

**MAKES ABOUT 1.5 KG (3½ LB)**

| | |
|---|---|
| **1 kg (2¼ lb) blueberries** | Rinse quickly in a colander, then put into a preserving pan and crush slightly. |
| **100 ml (3½ fl oz) water**<br>**a pinch of salt** | Add, and cook until soft and pulpy. |
| **finely grated zest and juice of 1 lemon**<br>**800 g (1¾ lb) caster sugar, warmed** | Add, stir together, and heat to dissolve the sugar. Boil for 5–10 minutes, or until setting point is reached. Test for setting point (see page 196). Pour into clean jars and seal. Store in a cool dark place. |

The jam is nicest if it has a soft set.

# CRANBERRY AND APPLE COMPOTE

**MAKES 1 KG (2¼ LB)**

| | |
|---|---|
| **500 g (18 oz) cranberries, washed**<br>**2 apples, peeled, cored and cut into sizeable chunks**<br>**1 cinnamon stick**<br>**2 pieces of lemon zest, removed with a potato peeler**<br>**juice of ½ lemon**<br>**juice of 1 orange**<br>**200 g (7 oz) caster sugar** | Place in a large pan, and heat, stirring occasionally, until the sugar dissolves.<br>Cook until the cranberries and the apple are soft, approximately 20–25 minutes.<br>Cool and keep covered in the refrigerator. |

Use as a jam or preserve, or serve with ice cream as a dessert.

From top: *Blueberry jam, Dried apricot and raisin preserve, and Cranberry and apple compote*

# Papaya Jam

**MAKES ABOUT 1 KG (2¼ LB)**

| | |
|---|---|
| **1 kg (2¼ lb) ripe papayas** | Cut in half and remove the seeds. Spoon out the soft ripe flesh and pass through a sieve. |
| **juice of 3 lemons** | Mix into the pulp. |
| **caster sugar** | Weigh the papaya and mix in the same amount of sugar.<br>Place in a heavy-based saucepan and heat to dissolve the sugar, then simmer for 10 minutes. Test for setting (see below). |
| **40 ml (1½ fl oz) rum (optional)** | If the jam is ready, season with rum (if using). Pour into clean jars whilst hot, and seal firmly.<br>Store in a cool dark place. |

To test for setting point, put 5 ml (1 teaspoon) of the hot mixture on to a saucer and allow to cool (in the freezer, for speed, if you like). If, when cool, the mixture crinkles when pushed with a finger, then the jam is ready. If it is still runny, continue to boil. Remove and test frequently, as the setting point can be passed in a few seconds. Each time, when testing, remove the mixture from the heat.

# Pine Needle Jelly

**MAKES ABOUT 1 KG (2¼ LB)**

| | |
|---|---|
| **100 g (4 oz) light green fir or spruce needles** | Rinse thoroughly in hot water and then in cold. Place in a large heavy-bottomed saucepan. |
| **1.2 litres (2 pints) water** | Pour in and bring to the boil. Simmer until the needles are almost without colour, about 30 minutes. Leave to drain overnight through muslin or a jelly bag into a bowl. |
| **caster sugar** | Measure the juice obtained and mix with the same |

| 30 ml (2 tablespoons) lemon juice | volume of sugar, plus the lemon juice.<br>Bring to the boil, and leave to simmer for 10–15 minutes. Test for setting (see left).<br>When ready, remove from the stove, pour into clean jars, and seal. Cool and store in a cool, dark place. |

 This confection does not turn to a jelly, remaining rather more the consistency of honey. This 'honey' comes from Switzerland, where I learned it was made by our neighbours in small quantities as a cure for coughs and colds!

# DRIED APRICOT AND RAISIN PRESERVE

### MAKES 500 G (18 OZ)

| 250 g (9 oz) dried apricots<br>1 litre (1¾ pints) water<br>juice of 2 oranges | Place in a saucepan and leave to soak overnight. |

| 1 cinnamon stick<br>1 vanilla pod, split | Add, and cook the mixture until the apricots are soft and pulpy, about 30–40 minutes. Add more water as and when required. Leave to cool. |

| 65 g (2½ oz) raisins<br>juice of 1 orange | Cover with water in a small pan and cook very gently until the raisins are soft and have absorbed most of the liquid. Drain and leave to cool.<br>Spoon the cooled apricot mixture into a liquidiser and coarsely blend. (For a softer, smoother texture, just add more water.)<br>Mix the apricot purée with the raisins. Cool thoroughly, place in a dish, and keep covered in the refrigerator. |

 Serve as a jam or spread, nicest on toasted brioche (see page 184). The apricots can also be left whole, not liquidised, and served as a dessert, wonderful with the Lemon Cheese Snow on page 166.
You can cook fresh apricots in much the same way, but the result will be much more liquid, more like a *coulis* than a compote.

# CHOCOLATE

The word 'chocoholic' has only recently been coined, but for years millions of people have been passionate about eating chocolate. This is not just a national indulgence in Britain, for virtually every country in Europe boasts its own chocolate industry and its own addicts. Apparently we Swiss are the champion chocolate eaters, consuming nearly 10 kg (22 lb) each per year (we also think our chocolate is the *best*), but the British, Germans, Belgians and Americans are not far behind. I am no chocoholic luckily, but I do enjoy the occasional chocolate treat!

Chocolate comes from the cacao tree which originates in Central and South America. The beans are removed from the large ridged pods and fermented on the ground for about six days. They are then roasted to dry the outer skin; this skin is then removed together with the germ leaving what are known as cocoa nibs. These are then ground to a thick chocolate paste; this is separated into cocoa butter (about 55 per cent of the paste), and chocolate liquor. The latter is basic unsweetened chocolate and, if pressed further, becomes cocoa powder.

All these chocolate refinements took place in the last 150 years or so. Only in 1828 did a Dutchman, Conrad van Houten, discover how to extract the cocoa butter; this was then utilised by the English firm of Fry to make eating chocolate. Thereafter, my compatriots took over; in 1876, a Swiss named Daniel Peter invented milk chocolate by using Nestlé's new dried milk.

The best chocolate to use in cooking is *couverture* or unsweetened chocolate: as it contains no sugar, it is too bitter for eating. This can be difficult to obtain, so look for dark, plain or semisweet chocolates; these contain chocolate liquor, additional cocoa butter and sugar. Milk chocolate contains dried milk as well as sugar. The best white chocolate is cocoa butter without any chocolate liquor so shouldn't, according to some, be called chocolate at all. Cocoa powder is as described, with no added milk powder or sugar, and

*A heart-shaped Chocolate truffle cake*

often is the easiest way of adding a chocolate flavour (*never* use drinking chocolate).

Chocolate is temperamental. To melt it for use in any of the following recipes, break it up into small pieces and place in a dry bowl over a pan or in a *bain-marie* of simmering water. Do not boil. If the recipe calls for it, add liquid to the chocolate and heat them both together; in this case the melting could be over direct, but still very gentle, heat.

Chocolate is obviously used most in sweet foods, but can also be used, surprisingly, in a few savoury dishes. Many of the best-known chocolate recipe names are not here – Black Forest Gâteau (Germany), Sachertorte (Austria), Florentines (Italy) and Devil's Food Cake (USA) – but I think there is enough of a choice to satisfy even the most ardent of chocoholics!

# CHOCOLATE TRUFFLE CAKE

**SERVES 10**

| | |
|---|---|
| **1 × 20–23 cm (8–9 in) chocolate sponge (see opposite)** | Slice an approximately 5 mm (¼ in) circle off the top of the sponge. Place this circle on a cake board. |
| **50 ml (2 fl oz) sugar syrup (see page 169)**<br>**50 ml (2 fl oz) rum** | Mix together and brush over the sponge circle. Arrange a flan ring the same diameter as the cake around the sponge circle on the board. |
| **250 g (9 oz) plain chocolate, broken into pieces** | Melt in a bowl over simmering water. |
| **375 ml (13 fl oz) whipping cream** | Whip to soft peaks.<br>Pour half the slightly cooled melted chocolate into the cream and mix well with a whisk. Add the remaining chocolate, and beat gently, but working quickly, until the mixture is homogeneous.<br>Pour the mixture into the flan ring and smooth the surface. Place in the refrigerator to set, about 30–60 minutes.<br>Lift the ring off carefully. |
| **20 g (¾ oz) cocoa powder** | Dust over the top of the cake. |

Serve the bulk of the sponge cake for tea or dessert with whipped cream, or wrap well and freeze.
To remove the ring neatly, wrap a hot towel round it for a couple of seconds, then rotate the ring slightly. This gives a smooth edge. (In professional kitchens, they use a blow torch!)
For special occasions, use a heart-shaped mould.

# Chocolate Sponge

**OVEN: Moderately hot to hot, 200–220°C/400–425°F/Gas 6–7**

Grease and flour a round 20–23 cm (8–9 in) tin with extra butter and flour. Shake out excess flour.

---

**75 g (3 oz) plain flour**
**15 g (½ oz) cocoa powder**
**15 g (½ oz) cornflour**

Sift together into a bowl.

---

**4 eggs**
**100 g (4 oz) caster sugar**

Whisk together with a balloon whisk in a bowl over a pan of hot water. Continue whisking until the mixture is light, creamy and has doubled in bulk. Remove from the heat and whisk until cold and thick or to the ribbon – when a ribbon-like trail forms on the surface of the mix when you trail some back into it off the whisk.
Fold in the flour mixture very gently.

---

**50 g (2 oz) unsalted butter or margarine, melted**

Fold in very gently. Place in the prepared tin and bake in the preheated oven for 30–40 minutes (see below). Turn out on to a cooling tray.

---

Test with a thin skewer; if it comes out dry, the cake is ready.

# Marbled Cake

**MAKES 1 CAKE**

**OVEN:** Moderate, 180°C/350°F/Gas 4

Grease and flour a 1.75 litre (3 pint) *kugelhopf* tin.

---

| | |
|---|---|
| **250 g (9 oz) unsalted butter**<br>**250 g (9 oz) vanilla sugar** | Cream together until pale and fluffy. |

---

| | |
|---|---|
| **4 large eggs, beaten** | Gradually beat in. |

---

| | |
|---|---|
| **250 g (9 oz) self-raising flour** | Fold in, then transfer half the mixture to another bowl. |

---

| | |
|---|---|
| **finely grated rind of 1 orange**<br>**40 g (1½ oz) raisins, soaked in 15 ml (1 tablespoon) dark rum** | Add to one mixture. |

---

| | |
|---|---|
| **30 ml (2 tablespoons) unsweetened cocoa powder, mixed with 15 ml (1 tablespoon) dark rum or water**<br>**65 g (2½ oz) plain chocolate, chopped into small pieces** | Add to the other mixture.<br>Put alternate spoonfuls of the two mixtures into the prepared tin. Tap gently to level the surface, then bake in the preheated oven for about 1 hour until well risen and firm to the touch. Turn out on to a wire rack to cool. |

---

A traditional *kugelhopf* is a rich sweet bread studded with raisins and almonds, coming from the Alsace region of France. The tin is shaped like a turban, with a hole in the centre. You can, of course, use an ordinary cake or loaf tin, or small individual tins.

Clockwise from top: *Chocolate brownies, Marbled cake slices, Wholewheat gingerbread and Marzipan and cranberry cake (see pages 182 and 183)*

# CHOCOLATE BROWNIES

**MAKES ABOUT 16 × 2.5 CM (1 IN) BROWNIES**

**OVEN:** Moderate, 180°C/350°F/Gas 4

| | |
|---|---|
| **100 g (4 oz)** unsweetened cooking chocolate, chopped | Place in a bowl over hot water and melt. Cool a little. |
| **50 g (2 oz) unsalted** butter, in small pieces | Add and stir until the butter has melted and blended with the chocolate. |
| **2 eggs** **175 g (6 oz) caster** sugar **5 ml (1 teaspoon)** vanilla essence | Beat together until fluffy, and blend into the chocolate and butter mixture. |
| **75 g (3 oz) plain flour** a good pinch each of baking powder and salt | Sift together, then fold into the mixture. |
| **50 g (2 oz) pecans or** walnuts, roughly chopped | Mix in. Pour the batter into a greased 20 cm (8 in) square baking tin and bake in the preheated oven for 20–25 minutes or until a skewer inserted just comes out clean. Allow to cool, then cut into squares – they will turn fudgy as they cool. |

To make marbled brownies, melt only 50 g (2 oz) chocolate, and set this aside. Melt the butter separately, and proceed as above until the flour and nuts have been folded into the butter and eggs. Divide the mixture in half, and add the melted chocolate to one half. Pour first the chocolate mixture, then the white mixture into the baking tin. Draw a knife through to 'marble' them, and bake as above.

# CHOCOLATE SOUFFLÉ

**SERVES 4**

**OVEN:** Moderately hot, 200°C/400°F/Gas 6

| | |
|---|---|
| 25 g (1 oz) soft unsalted butter<br>60 g (2¼ oz) caster sugar | Butter and dust eight small soufflé ramekins with about 30 ml (2 tablespoons) of the sugar. Knock excess sugar back into the bulk of the sugar. |
| 8 sponge fingers | Break into pieces and divide between the ramekins. |
| 45 ml (3 tablespoons) Grand Marnier | Divide between the ramekins. |
| 100 g (4 oz) bitter or plain chocolate | Chop and melt in a bowl over a pan of hot water. Remove from the heat. |
| 4 egg yolks | Stir into the chocolate. |
| 4 egg whites | Whip until they form soft peaks. |
| juice of ½ lemon | Add to the egg whites, and sprinkle in the remaining sugar. Continue to whip until stiff and glossy.<br>Stir about a quarter of the egg white into the chocolate mix to loosen it. Fold in the remainder.<br>Fill the prepared moulds with the soufflé mixture.<br>Run your thumb around the inside edge of each dish.<br>Bake in the preheated oven for 8–10 minutes. |
| icing sugar | Dust over the tops of the soufflés and serve immediately. |

Running one's thumb around the edges of the soufflés keeps the mixture away from the top edges of the ramekins, enabling it to rise easily and evenly.

# Chocolate Pecan Pie

**SERVES 8**

**OVEN:** Moderately hot, 200°C/400°F/Gas 6, then moderate, 180°C/350°F/Gas 4

| | |
|---|---|
| 1 quantity sweet pastry (see page 180) | Roll out the pastry, and use to line a 20 cm (8 in) tart tin. Line with foil, fill with baking beans, then bake blind in the preheated oven for 10 minutes. Remove the beans and foil and bake the flan case for another 6–7 minutes. Cool. Reduce the temperature of the oven. |
| 120 g (4½ oz) plain chocolate, chopped into small pieces 50 g (2 oz) unsalted butter | Melt together over a pan of hot water. |
| 4 eggs 230 ml (7½ fl oz) dark corn syrup, or maple syrup a few drops of vanilla essence | Whisk together, then blend in the melted chocolate. Mix well. |
| 250 g (9 oz) shelled pecan nuts | Stir in, then pour the mixture into the pastry case. Bake in the moderate oven for about 30 minutes until the tart has puffed slightly in the centre, and is just set. |
| icing sugar whipped cream | Serve warm with a dusting of icing sugar and some whipped cream. |

**M** Small pies can be made as well.

*Chocolate pecan pies, large and small*

# CHOCOLATE TUILES

**MAKES ABOUT 12**

**OVEN:** Moderate, 180°C/350°F/Gas 4

| | |
|---|---|
| **40 g (1½ oz) light brown sugar**<br>**60 g (2¼ oz) granulated sugar**<br>**3 egg whites** | Whisk together in a bowl. |

| | |
|---|---|
| **50 g (2 oz) plain flour**<br>**15 ml (1 tablespoon) cocoa powder**<br>**a pinch of salt and powdered cinnamon**<br>**5 ml (1 teaspoon) finely grated orange zest** | Add, and stir well until blended. |

| | |
|---|---|
| **15 ml (1 tablespoon) orange juice**<br>**30 ml (2 tablespoons) double cream**<br>**60 g (2¼ oz) unsalted butter, melted** | Add, and stir in. Let the mixture rest for approximately 15–20 minutes.<br>Spoon out on to a greased baking tray, and spread it out lightly from the centre, making neat 6–7.5 cm (2½–3 in) circles. Only make two or three at a time as the batter will spread.<br>Bake for approximately 6–7 minutes in the preheated oven. The tuiles should just have slightly darkened at the edges.<br>Remove from the oven, let rest on the tray for about 30 seconds, then lift off with a large spatula. Drape over a rolling pin while still warm to shape into curls. Continue making until all the batter has been used up. Bake, rest and shape the remainder in the same way. Leave to cool. |

Store in a rigid container to avoid breakages.
These tuiles are good for afternoon tea, but also delicious served as *petits fours*.

# CHOCOLATE PRALINE PARFAIT

### SERVES ABOUT 12

**50 g (2 oz) raisins**
**30 ml (2 tablespoons) brandy**

Soak together for 15-20 minutes.

---

**100 g (4 oz) almonds, toasted**
**50 g (2 oz) dark chocolate, melted**

Mix together with the raisins. Spread out on to greaseproof paper and leave to set in the refrigerator. Turn out and roughly chop.

---

**9 egg yolks**
**75 g (3 oz) caster sugar**

Whisk together in a bowl over hot water until light and frothy.
Remove from the heat and water.

---

**100 g (4 oz) dark chocolate, melted**
**25 g (1 oz) cocoa powder, sifted**
**120 g (4½ oz) praline paste**

Slowly mix into the egg yolk mixture, and cool slightly if still warm.

---

**600 ml (1 pint) double cream, whipped**

Fold in along with the almond mixture. Pour into a 1.5 litre (2½ pint) terrine mould and leave to set in the freezer until firm – at least 4 hours.
Turn out, cut in portions, and serve with chocolate sauce (see page 213).

---

Praline paste is an almond-based chocolate, available in good stores.

# CHRISTIAN'S CHOCOLATE STRAWBERRY SLICE

**SERVES 8**

**OVEN:** Hot, 220°C/425°F/Gas 7

| | |
|---|---|
| ½ **quantity Chocolate Puff Pastry (overleaf)** | Roll out into a thin rectangular sheet 26 × 18 cm (10½ × 7 in). Place on a greased baking tray and allow to rest in a cold place for 1 hour. Bake in the preheated oven for 10–15 minutes. Turn the sheet over and bake for another 5 minutes. |
| **3 egg yolks** <br> **50 g (2 oz) caster sugar** | To make the pastry cream, whisk together to a fluffy texture. |
| **30 g (1¾ oz) plain flour** | Add and mix in well. |
| **250 ml (8 fl oz) milk** <br> **½ vanilla pod, split** | Bring to the boil together. Pour into the egg mixture and mix well. Pour the mixture back into the pan and bring back to the boil, whisking continuously. Remove from the heat, and strain into a clean bowl. |
| **15 ml (1 tablespoon) caster sugar** | Sprinkle over to prevent a skin forming. Cool. Cut the pastry sheet into three equal pieces. Whisk the pastry cream to a smooth thick batter. |
| **150 g (5 oz) double cream** | Whip until about half-whipped, and fold into the pastry cream. Spread a thick layer of this cream on to one sheet of pastry. |
| **about 400 g (14 oz) strawberries, hulled** | Cut in half if large. Arrange half in a layer on top of the cream. Fill any gaps with more pastry cream. Place the second sheet of pastry on top and repeat the pastry cream and strawberry procedure once again. Finish with the last pastry layer, and trim. |
| **icing sugar** | Sprinkle over the top, slice and serve. |

*Christian's chocolate strawberry slice*

# CHOCOLATE PUFF PASTRY

### MAKES ABOUT 450 G (1 LB)

**200 g (7 oz) strong plain flour**
**a pinch of salt**

Sieve together.

---

**200 g (7 oz) unsalted butter**

Rub 30 g (1¼ oz) of the butter into the flour, then make a well in the centre.

---

**a few drops of lemon juice**
**120 ml (4 fl oz) ice-cold water**

Add and knead well into a smooth dough in a ball shape. Relax the dough in a cool place for approximately 30 minutes.

---

**30 ml (2 tablespoons) cocoa powder**

Mix with the remaining butter, and shape back into a small block of about 8 cm (3¼ in) square. Chill.
Cut a cross halfway through the dough and pull out the corners to form a star shape. Roll out the points of the star, leaving the centre thick.
Flatten the cocoa butter until the same size as the centre piece of the dough. Place on the centre square. Fold over the flaps.
Roll the pastry out to a rectangle of about 15 cm (6 in) long and 7.5 cm (3 in) wide, keeping the corners square.
Fold the pastry rectangle in three from top and bottom like a business letter, then turn the dough 90° to bring the last folded side to your left. Gently press the open folds with the rolling pin to seal. This completes the first turn. Repeat the whole procedure – rolling out to a rectangle, folding in three and turning to complete a second turn. Mark the number of turns by pressing your finger tip into one corner. Cover and allow to rest for 20 minutes. Give the pastry four more turns allowing to rest between each turn. Use as required.

---

It is important that the fat is not too soft as it will melt and ooze out. If too hard, it will break through the paste when rolled. The pastry will freeze well. Defrost thoroughly, and allow to come back to room temperature before rolling.

# CHOCOLATE CHIP COOKIES

**MAKES ABOUT 24 COOKIES**

**OVEN:** Moderate, 180°C/350°F/Gas 4

75 g (3 oz) self-raising flour
50 g (2 oz) wholemeal flour
50 g (2 oz) soft brown sugar
50 g (2 oz) vanilla sugar
75 g (3 oz) soft unsalted butter
1 egg

Place in a food processor and process for a few seconds until just combined.

---

50 g (2 oz) walnuts, chopped
65 g (2½ oz) good chocolate, chopped in very small pieces

Mix in.
Use a spoon to drop small mounds of the mixture on to a greased baking sheet, keeping them well spaced out.
Bake the cookies in the preheated oven for approximately 10–12 minutes until they turn golden. Lift the cookies off the sheet, and place them on a wire rack to cool.

---

You could use flavourings other than chocolate if you like – try poppy seeds or diced dried apricot.

# CHOCOLATE SAUCE

120 g (4½ oz) good dark chocolate, chopped small
175 ml (6 fl oz) water

Place in a small saucepan and bring gently to the boil to melt.

---

75 g (3 oz) cocoa powder
75 g (3 oz) caster sugar
75 ml (2½ fl oz) water

Mix together to a thick paste.
Mix the two mixtures together, bring to the boil and cool.

---

This sauce can be served cold, whereas the previous sauce must be served warm. Both sauces serve six people.

# HONEY-BAKED NUTTY PEARS WITH HOT FUDGE SAUCE

**SERVES 6**

**OVEN:** Moderate, 180°C/350°F/Gas 4

| | |
|---|---|
| 6 fairly ripe pears | Peel, but keep the stems intact. Remove the cores with a corer from the bottom end of the pears. |
| 50 g (2 oz) each of hazelnuts and almonds, roasted and finely chopped<br>2 dried apricots, soaked and finely chopped<br>15 ml (1 tablespoon) apricot jam<br>Amaretto liqueur to taste | Mix together, adding the Amaretto to taste, and stuff into the pears. Pack in firmly. |
| a little unsalted butter | Arrange the pears in a well-buttered dish, just large enough to hold them. |
| 120 g (4½ oz) honey<br>100 ml (3½ fl oz) orange juice<br>juice of 1 lemon<br>100 ml (3½ fl oz) water<br>2 cloves | Combine in a saucepan, bring to the boil, then pour over the pears. Cover the dish, and bake in the preheated oven for approximately 40–50 minutes until the pears are tender but not mushy. Baste with the juices every 10 minutes. |
| 1 quantity Hot Fudge Sauce (see previous page) | Serve the pears warm with some of their juices and the hot sauce. |

**M** You could also simply poach the pears, unstuffed, and serve them with some hot fudge sauce as well as a little white chocolate sauce (sweeten a runny custard with white chocolate to taste).

*Honey-baked nutty pears with hot fudge sauce*

# HOT FUDGE SAUCE

| | |
|---|---|
| **75 g (3 oz) unsalted butter** | Melt in a small saucepan. |
| **25 g (1 oz) cocoa powder** | Add, and whisk until smooth. |
| **30 g (1¼ oz) unsweetened chocolate, chopped**<br>**150 g (5 oz) granulated sugar**<br>**85 ml (3 fl oz) evaporated milk** | Stir in and bring the sauce to a boil over medium heat, stirring all the while. Remove immediately from the heat. |
| **a pinch of salt** | Stir in and allow to cool slightly. |
| **vanilla essence** | Add a few drops and mix well. |

# WHITE CHOCOLATE ICE CREAM

**SERVES 10**

**MAKES APPROX 1 LITRE (1¾ PINTS)**

| | |
|---|---|
| **250 g (9 oz) white chocolate** | Chop and melt in a bowl over a *bain-marie* of hot water. |
| **250 ml (9 fl oz) each of milk and double cream**<br>**½ vanilla pod, split** | Heat together gently, then bring to the boil. |
| **4 egg yolks** | Whisk until starting to go pale.<br>Slowly whisk the boiling milk into the egg yolks, then return the mixture to the saucepan, and cook over a low heat, stirring all the time, until the mixture coats the back of the spoon.<br>Strain the custard into the melted chocolate and blend well, then leave to cool.<br>Churn and freeze in a *sorbetière*; or place in a mould or container, freeze for 3–4 hours in the freezer, taking out once or twice and beating to disperse any ice particles. |

Make a dark chocolate ice cream in virtually the same way, using bitter or dark chocolate instead of white. Whisk 25 g (1 oz) caster sugar with the egg yolks; and stir in at the end 15 ml (1 tablespoon) orange liqueur and the juice and finely grated zest of 1 orange.

You could make a chocolate bombe with these two ice creams. Double the quantity of the dark, and use to line a freezer-proof bowl. Freeze until set to a dark shell. Fill with the white ice cream and return to the freezer to harden. Dip the bowl into hot water quickly then turn the bombe out on to a serving dish.

# CHOCOLATE SORBET

**SERVES 10**

| | |
|---|---|
| **200 g (7 oz) caster sugar**<br>**25 g (1 oz) cocoa powder**<br>**30 g (1¼ oz) plain dark chocolate, broken into small pieces**<br>**a pinch of salt**<br>**600 ml (1 pint) water**<br>**½ cinnamon stick** | Place in a suitable, thick-bottomed saucepan, bring to a gentle boil, and simmer for 3-5 minutes. Strain. |
| **100 ml (3½ fl oz) espresso coffee** | Add to the mixture, then leave to cool.<br>Churn and freeze in a *sorbetière*; or place in a mould or container, and freeze as in the previous recipe. |

# CHERRY TRUFFLES

| | |
|---|---|
| **50 g (2 oz) dark chocolate**<br>**100 g (4 oz) milk chocolate** | Chop, then melt together in a bowl over hot water. Leave to cool a little. |
| **120 g (4½ oz) unsalted butter**<br>**100 g (4 oz) icing sugar** | Heat together until creamy, then gradually beat into the cooled melted chocolate. |
| **45 ml (3 tablespoons) cherry brandy**<br>**45 ml (3 tablespoons) cocoa powder** | Add and work gradually into the cream mixture. Chill.<br>Put mixture into a piping bag and using a small round nozzle, squeeze out small truffles on to a tray. |
| **cocoa powder** | Place on a plate and roll the truffles quickly in it. Store in a cool place. |

# CHOCOLATE TRUFFLES

| | |
|---|---|
| **250 g (9 oz) dark, milk or white chocolate, broken into pieces** | Melt over a pan or *bain-marie* of hot water, stirring occasionally until melted. Remove from the heat and water. |
| **75 ml (5 tablespoons) double cream** | Bring to the boil, then cool to tepid. Trickle into the melted chocolate and mix the two together well. |
| **vanilla essence, brandy, Cointreau or Grand Marnier to taste** | Add flavouring of choice (no more than a few drops). Whisk the paste until it becomes lighter in colour and fluffy. Leave in a cool place until it has thickened, about 5-10 minutes, and has become firm. |
| **cocoa powder, icing sugar or chopped nuts to coat** | Take a teaspoonful of the mixture and place on a tray. Dust your hands or fingertips with cocoa or sugar and quickly roll each piece to form a ball. If it becomes too soft too quickly, place back in the refrigerator for another 5 minutes. Roll in a coating of nuts, cocoa or sugar, place in paper cases, chill and serve. |

# TEA SWEETS

| | |
|---|---|
| **50 g (2 oz) unsalted butter**<br>**2 egg yolks**<br>**100 g (4 oz) caster sugar** | Mix together until creamy. |
| **250 ml (8 fl oz) water**<br>**45–50 ml (3 heaped tablespoons) tealeaves of choice** | Bring the water to the boil, add the tealeaves and brew for 6 minutes. Strain and cool. |
| **300 g (11 oz) dark chocolate, chopped**<br>**5 ml (1 teaspoon) finely** | Meanwhile, melt together in a bowl over hot water, and leave to become cool. Mix the strong tea mixture into the butter mixture, |

| grated orange zest | followed by the chocolate mixture. Leave to chill for several hours. Form into small balls. |

| cocoa powder | Place on a plate and roll the balls in it. Store in a cool place. |

# CANDIED CHOCOLATE ORANGE PEEL

| 3 large oranges | Using a small sharp knife, make four slits from top to bottom at quarterly intervals around the oranges. Remove the peel. Place peel into a pan, cover with plenty of boiling water, and simmer for approximately 10 minutes. Refresh in cold water, then repeat the boiling and refreshing process twice more. |

| 500 g (18 oz) caster sugar <br> 1 litre (1¾ pints) water <br> 2 slices fresh ginger | Combine in a heavy-bottomed suacepan, and cook until the sugar has dissolved. Add the drained peel and mix it well with the syrup. Cook very slowly for about 1-1½ hours, until the peel is soft. <br> Remove the peel and place on a wire rack to drain and dry. Sprinkle with extra sugar and leave overnight. If not coating straightaway, store in a tightly lidded jar. |

| 100 g (4 oz) dark chocolate, melted | To coat with chocolate, cut the peel into thin batons. Taking one baton at a time, dip half of it into the melted chocolate. Lay on greaseproof paper until dry and set. Serve as a *petit four*. |

# INDEX

Page numbers in *italic* refer to the illustrations

I should like to express my
thanks to the following for
their help and support: Kit
Chan, David Wilson, Melanie
Davis, Tom Belshaw, Jane
Suthering, Susan Fleming,
Shelley–Anne Claircourt,
Deirdre Connor, and Ray Neve
and the Kitchen Brigade.

**Anton Mosimann**